Do More Better Faster

The Optimal Outcomes Approach
on
How to be More Productive
and
Get More Done in Less Time

Dan Kristoph

TABLE OF CONTENTS

YOUR FREE GIFT

As a way to say thank you for reading one of my books, I offer you my free e-book with the title "**23 Good Habits in Life: The Simple Routine Practices that Can Make You More Positive, Happy, and Successful**". It is an e-book with more than 80-pages content which talks about why good habits can be important to make you a more positive, happy, and successful person, what are the things that can define good and bad habits in life, and 23 good habits that are simple yet impactful. Reading this e-book might be what you just need to kickstart the implementation of more good habits and less bad habits in your life.

To grab your copy, you can visit the link given below and join my email list:
https://positivitystories.com/free-gift

*The Simple Routine Practices that
Can Make You More Positive,
Happy, and Successful*

Dan Kristoph

In the following pages, we will discuss many things about productivity: What are the importance of productivity in our lives, the five things that are needed to implement high productivity in work, and the Do More Better Faster approach which, if applied correctly, should result in getting much more done with less time for you.

Curious about the book content? Without further ado, let us start with the discussion in the first part of the book.

FOREWORD: LESS INPUT VS MORE OUTPUT?

Productivity is the holy grail of our work.

It is something that everyone wants when they put in the effort on something. Because by having high productivity, we should be able to achieve more with less from our work.

It seems pretty obvious that we work because we want to gain something from the process, whatever that something is. When the condition is impossible to get the results that we want, then we will not have any motivation to do our work.

Either as an employee or someone who owns a business, there are short-term and long-term objectives that we want to achieve by using the medium of our work. You are an employee? Then probably in the short-term, you want to work hard on something that you do so you can submit it to your boss on time and receive an excellent assessment because of the quality of the result. In the long-term, you probably want to use the consistent result of good results from your work so you can get a promotion to the managerial level in your company. If you happen to do business, then your short-term objectives possibly are creating and launching a great product while also have an excellent marketing plan for it. The long-term objectives could be that you want to have excellent annual sales for the new product and making your business profit more significantly. Every one of us has something that we want to attain from the work that we do, either in our near or long-term future.

By having the right kind of productivity, we should be able to get our targets or even exceed them in a shorter time.

That, of course, makes a high productivity a great thing for us. Achieving more with fewer resources needed is also important because the time when we achieve the big success that we want in life solely depends on that.

When you want to achieve success, you need to work until you get it. That is one important thing that we should keep in mind. Success is usually a product of cumulative hard work that is done in a long period. If we can accomplish more results in the shortest duration of our work, then logically we should be able to achieve all the things that we want from our work as soon as it can be.

Now, who does not want to achieve life success in the shortest time possible? Some of the things that we want the most to come much earlier in our life? That is something that all of us should want to get in the work that we do!

However, it might not be that easy to achieve success in the earliest that we can by utilizing the highest productivity that we are able to in our work. There is always something that seems to be able to block us to do that. Either it is the distraction that we receive from external sources, the unfocused work that we do because something else that bothers our mind besides the current work that we do, or probably the urge of procrastination that often comes when we seriously want to do something. These things are just a few examples of problems that can make us unproductive and cannot optimize the time that we have in our working hours well.

There are also the things that we must allocate our time too besides work. Personal matters like doing some activities with our family and friends or refreshing activities after work like just resting or unwind ourselves to release the stress that we have got during our work are important for us too. They take time in our daily schedule and make us need to condense our time to fit them all with the work that we have to do. Sometimes, those things besides the work that we do take a larger part too compared with the working hours that we allocate for our daily schedule.

These other things besides work that also needs our attention can make us feel that we do not have enough time to work. We might even feel that there are too many sacrifices that we have to take so we can achieve the results that we want from our work. That can make us unmotivated to give our best in the effort to produce those desired results.

Too Much Sacrifice for The Result?
Have you ever felt tired because you think that the job that you do is never completed and there are always more things that you need to do so you can produce the results that you want?

All of us may already have some experiences like that before. Like, the project that you have to finish needs revision over and over again so that you can satisfy the requirements from your boss or your customers. Or the sales target that seems so hard to achieve. Whatever you do seem to not make you get closer to that result that you want from the product/service that you sell in your business.

Things like these sucks big time and can make us feel very frustrated or stressed. You might feel that you have already given the maximum effort that you can in your work but still, the outcome that you want is not attained yet. There is always extra work to do before you have the chance to get what you want from your work.

There seem to be too many things that you have to sacrifice in your work? Perhaps. This can bring down your motivation to give your best at work because you feel that you always have to push yourselves harder to get the optimum results.

There can be some logic too why this has to happen. It is hard to get our work right from the first time that we try it, especially if we are new to the area of work. We still do not have enough experience in doing things correctly so we might happen to stumble into a thing or two during our effort. It seems that only after we have accumulated enough experience in the work that we do, we can navigate our way well in it.

However, how long should we work until we can do that? How much should we give into our work until we reach the point where we have accumulated enough experience?

There is a concept of 10,000 hours rule that is popularized by Malcolm Gladwell in his book *Outlier*. This concept says that basically, you have to collect 10,000 hours of doing something so you can gain enough experience to say that you have the mastery of the thing that you do your work on. If we take that we work in all of the 52 weeks in a year with 5 working days each week and 8 hours each day, then it means that we need to roughly work consistently for 5 years so we can achieve that 10,000 hours target. That is if we can work in all 52 weeks, 5 days a week, and 8 hours a day in all of the 5 years as we usually have other things that we have to do besides work that disrupt our progress. Counting that, it may take us even more years from the 5 years standard to fulfill the 10,000 hours rule.

Sounds long enough? You bet it is. Probably most of us do not want to sacrifice that much time to achieve the mastery that has been theorized especially if we are not forced to work on the thing (e.g. it is not the job which gives the main income for us). After all, we will need to sacrifice time, mind, effort, or any other resources that might be relevant to our work and we have to do that for years. That is before talking about chasing the success that we want to achieve after the mastery which is gained from our work.

It seems that the optimal way for that is achieving more results with less sacrifice that we need to do for our work. However, more results in the work that we do might not be always good for us and should be careful with that basic thought.

More Results are Better?

There might be some works that we do every day in our working hours which can give different kinds of results for us. For example, in one working day, you might participate in a meeting for a project, analyze the data that you have got in your computer for the report that you want to present to your boss, and go to a branch of your company to check about the sales and promotion activity that has run there. Those activities might be done to give progress in different kinds of works and you feel that you must attend all of them to do your job right in the company.

However, you might want to think again: are all the results of those works needed for the job that you have to do? The meeting that you attend in one period that day is probably not that necessary for you to be present there. It may just talk about another side of the project that you have little to no involvement about. You might just need to talk to your peer after the meeting to know about the update on that side of the project and do not need to participate fully in the meeting from start to finish. The audit that you do for the business activity that is done in one of the company's branch is probably not needed because it can be done from the data that has been sent regularly by the branch. So, you just have to check it there for the things that you want to see from the sales and promotional activity results. The thing is the outcomes that you want from two of the activities that you allocate a considerable amount of your time on that day might be had without you have to do some work on them. The time that you have spent for those works might be better to be spent on the data analysis for the report that you do so it can be done better and faster or for some other things that need more of your direct work in them.

So, do more results in the work that you do directly translate to better performance and higher productivity? Not really in some instances. It might be the case that you need to be more selective on the results that you want to achieve from your works so they can be more meaningful for the targets that you have and the resources that you have spent on them. Those results might be unneeded because there are already other things that can compensate for them.

Thus, what can we infer about this? More results do not necessarily translate into better productivity and great progress in our work, it seems. You might want to reflect again for the improvement of work effectiveness and efficiency that you target in your work.

Job Effectivity and Efficiency
Effectivity and efficiency are important in terms of the productivity that you want to achieve in your work. By definition, implementing effectivity in work means that you have done the essential things only in your work, and having effectiveness means that you have utilized your work inputs well to produce the outputs that you want. As those definitions are related to what has been described before, high productivity means that you should be able to have effectiveness and efficiency too in your work. The work that you do needs to be essential in terms of producing the right output which is not redundant for you while its process can

also use your resources as little as possible to produce the output that you want as many as possible.

That can be hard, of course. In terms of effectivity, we might find it difficult to recognize the job that we need to do versus the job which is redundant and can be removed to make more space for other works that are more relevant for us. At the present moment, we might already trap ourselves in the usual work habit that we do which can take a lot of effort for us to modify. It can be also that we find it difficult to turn down the redundant works that have been assigned for us to attend to by our peers or supervisor. The meeting that we do not need to attend might be something that we want to avoid to improve our effectivity. However, the invitation from our peers to join the meeting can be hard to ignore. Those things can make us go back against the commitment to realize high productivity in our working hours.

When we look at the efficiency thing, there are a lot of things too which can halt us in terms of having a high efficiency in our work. One resource which is crucial for us in our work is time and we have already talked about the things that can make us run out of enough time to allocate into the work that we do. When we work, the things might also distract our mind into giving focus completely for our work. Things like other matters besides work that we care about or unclear focus can bring many problems in terms of efficiency. We can do the opposite of work efficiency instead, which is having put a large input of resources for our work but gaining a little result. That can be bad for the quality of work results that we want to achieve and when we will even get something that can be counted as a result of our work. Do not even start to talk about mastery or success in our work as it is so far away from us because of the low efficiency that we have in our work.

Having low efficiency and effectiveness in our job automatically means that we have low productivity too. This translates to a much longer time than we need in our work to achieve success. It is clearly something that we do not want.

So, for every one of us that works, it is important to know what is the way to achieve high efficiency, effectivity, and, in turn, high productivity. We need to push ourselves hard in that way so we can work on something that produces much more results with better quality and faster time. Do more, better, and faster. But what is that way that we need to know and push hard for to achieve high productivity in our work? Well, this book is written to try to give the answer on that question for you.

The Book Structure
To be able to give comprehensive but practical solutions for high productivity in work, this book will try to deepen your thought about the importance of doing work in a more, better, and faster way, the kind of mentality that we need to have to optimally do it, and some tips that you can practice to do more better faster. The approach that is used in this book is the Do, More, Better, and Faster approaches which will be deeply discussed separately in the next chapters of the book. As such, the book chapters are being organized as follows:

Why We Need to Do More, Better, and Faster? – This chapter will give the why for us in our quest to achieve productivity by doing things in a Do More Better Faster passion. It will emphasize the importance of time shortening focus in our work without neglecting the quality of our work results.

Five Things We Need to Do More Better Faster Optimally – The Do, More, Better, and Faster approaches that we will do our work in needs to have a certain mindset and mentality from us so we can do it optimally. This part highlights what are the five aspects of mindset and mentality that we need to pay attention to so the approaches can be implemented in work.

Do: No More Work Excuses – The Do approach tries to significantly improve the motivation that we have to do our work optimally. Five practical Do approach tips will be described in detail to help us with that.

More: No More Unoptimized Effort – More approach puts in the effort to work on more tasks at the same amount of time that we have. As with the Do, five practical tips that can be directly implemented will be given to support ourselves in improving this More part of our work.

Better: No More Redundant Tasks – As being noted in the foreword, we must do the essential work to gain the essential result. This Better part of the book will try to handle this for you with tips being given also to make your work stay on the correctly focused lane.

Faster: No More Slow Execution – Time is a very important factor in our lives and the success that we want should be gained as soon as possible. Therefore, this Fast approach will focus on how can we make our tasks be completed in a faster fashion.

High productivity can be gained as long as we approach our work with the right mindset and the correct approach. There are some tips which we can practice in our work to help us with that and they will be given in this book so you know how you can optimize the time that you have to produce optimum results in your work that are meaningful for your success.

Curious to know more? Well, let's begin with the why part of the book that describes the importance of the high productivity approach.

WHY WE NEED TO DO MORE, BETTER, AND FASTER?

Work activities can be taxing to our energy and bring frustration to our mind. This can be amplified when we face bad situations in our work in which we need to struggle heavily.

Have you ever faced a trying moment in the work that you do? Probably you have tried your best in a project that you are mainly responsible for but the project fails spectacularly to produce the results that you and your company want. Perhaps you need to do a very difficult job in your work as an employee or at your business that makes you want to bang your head to the wall because of the high amount of stress that it causes to you. Possibly the people that you supervise their work for cannot seem to do it right no matter how much guidance that you have given to them. Those examples and a lot of different kinds of bad moments can make you go crazy with the work that you have to do.

When we need to solve the work problems that seem to be pretty hard, we tend to be in a bad mood. Especially, if the work has massive pressure on it because it defines some important things for you that makes you highly depend on its results or because of the high expectation that your supervisors or peers have in it. The pressure can add more frustration for you and it can be the hard time that you need to experience at some point during work. The bad mood that you have also do not help with things as it can even distract you from doing the best in your work.

There can be bad moments for us in our work when we do not feel motivated to put in the effort to finish it. However, it is important for us not to abandon the job because the things that we want as a result will not happen if we do not complete the job.

Everyone wants something from their work results. Surely you do not do your job just because you want to do it. Most of us do our main job because of the financial support that it can give to us. Either you are an employee or someone that works for yourself, the money that you get from your work surely cannot be ignored as one of the main things that motivate you to do your work. There can be also other things that can motivate you in your work such as the social impact that you want to give as a result of your work, the proud feeling that you can have when you accomplish something great in the work that you do, or probably the improved relationship that you can have with the people around you when you do your job satisfyingly. These things are the ones that should keep you to do your work even though there might be heavy struggles that you meet during the process.

And you must keep the motivation from the things that you want from your work results strong. Because if you do not have it, then you can easily find yourself do other things which are completely unrelated to your work. Losing the motivation to work and not doing it anymore surely have a bad impact on the things that you want from your work results.

Besides, we also have something bigger that we want to chase in life, don't we? It is the life success that we want to have from the work that we do. Something that we aspire to be but sometimes it seems so difficult to achieve because of the amount of work that we need to do to realize it. If we have struggles in the regular work that we do and refuse to continue doing it because of the struggles, then how can we ever hope to achieve something much bigger from our work?

What We Are Meant to Be

Let's go deeper to something big that you want to chase in life. What is the definition of life success for you?

There can be many different answers from a lot of people for this question. Your definition of success might be becoming a rich person who can buy anything, have a massive social impact for people around you, or some other things that can be considered as a great achievement personally if you finally realize it. Some of us might have already dreamed about it for a long time as achieving it is something that is very meaningful to us.

One thing that is similar to all of us regarding the success that we want to achieve despite the different definitions of it, though. It is that we must do some real hard work to achieve the success, especially if the definition of our success something that is still far away from the current condition that we have now. The work that we must do might be different depending on the success definition that we have in our life. But the important thing is that the work that we need to do for it most probably has a very high amount attached to it and it must be done consistently until we can accomplish what we want.

The thing is, as has been described earlier, it can be already hard for us to accomplish the regular work that we have to do without targeting the success that we want too much. If we add the success as the thing that we want to pursue on top of that, then aren't the struggles that we need to endure will be much bigger than the ones that we have already experienced in our work?

That truly might be the case, especially if the success that we want to achieve is in the different area from the main job that we do. For a simple example, you might still work as an employee in a company while your dream is to have a highly successful business on your own. When you have something like that then it can only mean two choices for you if you seriously want to achieve the accomplishment of having that successful business. Either you quit your job and focus your work fully on building the business until it can succeed or you work on some side business while still keeping your job as an employee. Both of these choices require you to work extra as it is not easy for someone to build a business from the ground up until it can achieve success.

It can be not so smooth for us when we seriously chase the success that we want as there can be failure events that we must experience during our progress. The failures can be hard to navigate and they can seriously test the resolve that we have regarding the achievements that we want to accomplish. We need to maintain our motivation so we can overcome the bad situation and keep the continuation of our success chase.

However, whatever the events that we experience to realize the success that we are meant to be, the key here is that we should still have a lot of work to do. If you get good progress in your work, then you should still keep working until you gain the success that you want. Even more so if you fail or meet struggles along the way. You need to work harder to come back up from the bad situation. Well, even if you have achieved success, you might still need to keep working so you can maintain or even improve the condition of success that you already have.

Work is the keyword here when you want to achieve success and it is true whatever the definition of success that you have or whatever the conditions that you want yourself to be in the future. When you want to work, then the most important thing to have seems to be related to our time resources. You cannot work if you do not have the time to do it. In fact, when you think about it, it might be the only essential element that you need to achieve success.

The Precious Time

All of us only have limited time to do anything that we want in a day. There can be only 24 hours for whoever we are and it is up to each of us to utilize the time that we have as optimal as possible for our cause.

Regarding the work that we do, it usually takes a significant portion of our time in a day. The more workload that we have, then logically we have to allocate more of our time if we want to sort it out.

For the success that we want to chase, it usually takes a lot of work to realize it. That means we have to allocate a lot of time for doing the work. Looking at the success stories from successful people, it can take years of consistent hard work before we can achieve the success that we want and that is a lot of time that we have to sacrifice in our side. Therefore, we must be able to utilize the time that we have optimally to do the work so the progress to our success can be much faster.

Time is a precious commodity and we must treat it as such every day. The more time that you allocate to something, the more you usually be able to produce from it. Everyone starts from zero in all of the things that they do in life. It is by the experience that they accumulate and the learnings that they have along with the work which they do that they can produce something meaningful. Nobody starts their work by already becoming adept and having success in it.

From the starting point until the point where you can achieve your success, there are many things that you must do and that means much time that you have to spend to be able to do them. Success requires you to spend some period on it and nobody knows exactly how much time you need. Of course, we hope that it is a short period before we can reach our goals but it can take much longer than we expect it to be. The certain thing is that as long as you do not allocate some time to work on the things that you have to do related to your chase of success, then you will never be able to succeed.

So, you must question yourself: have you allocated enough time to your work to achieve success? Well, the more that you spend your time on your work, the closer you should be to the success that you want. When you work to achieve success, you must make sure too that you have been highly productive with the time that you have. If you work with, for instance, your mind focuses on some other things that are unrelated to the work activity, then that most probably means that you have not utilized your time to work highly and that can make it longer for you to achieve the success that you want.

Being unproductive means that you do not use your time resource as good as possible. That can only bring disadvantage to you as that means that you should work much longer to compensate for the time that you spend being unproductive at work. Therefore, you must know how to do your work more, better, and faster in the time that you have so you can achieve the highest productivity that you can be for your work.

Time might be the only thing that you need for success thus what you do to utilize it is important to be what you aspire to. Other things that you still do not have and you think are crucial for the outcomes that you want to achieve can be had as long as you allocate your time to try to have it.

Everything Else Seems Does Not Matter

Now, what do you think that you lack at the moment to start working on your success other than time? The capital to build your business, the network that has an important connection for the success, the knowledge and skills to produce an excellent result for your work, or maybe the much-needed experience that you think you need to produce the right results from your work? Well, the fact is, those things that might halt you to start your work should be able to be accumulated as long as you provide your time for it.

You lack the money that you think you need to start chasing your success? Then you should think about the way to do it with the finance that you can spare. Look at the relevant resources that you already have and think about what kind of utilization that you can do with those resources so you can begin to work. The important thing here is to start first and as long as you allocate the time to work on it, then you should be able to secure the finance that you need to optimally work at some point in the future.

That is the same too for network, knowledge, skills, experience, or other factors that might be suspected to be the most important resources that you need for success. Do with what you already have to start and procure them along the way as you progress. If you do not start working, then the right moment when you have all the things that you think you need to start working for success might not come at all. The right time is now as some people say.

However, the one factor that you absolutely need for success is time and the work that goes along with it that you allocate your time for work. As long as you do not have the time for work, then you will not be able to have the chance to succeed in achieving the things that you desire.

So, the only thing that you need for success is the time that you need to do your work and high productivity brings a big impact on the time that you spend. By having the high productivity in your work, then you should be able to shorten the time that you need significantly without compromising your work results quality. You should be able also to work on the things that are relevant to your success because of the implementation of the right productivity. Remember this. Even if you have worked in the most effective and efficient way possible, working on the wrong things means that you are unproductive in relation to the success that you want to accomplish.

This means that you need to do more, better, and faster in the work that you do to achieve what you want as soon as possible. Now, what kind of mindset that you need so you can give that kind of high-quality work a chance and what are the things that you need to have in your mindset so you can improve your chance of doing high productivity work? Well, we will try to dive deeper into the discussion of this in the next chapters.

FIVE THINGS WE NEED TO DO MORE BETTER FASTER OPTIMALLY

If you want to do more, better, and faster in your work to achieve high productivity, then you should have the mindset which enables you to do your work optimally. Having the desire to be more productive while you are lazy to do your work is not going to cut it.

The things that you have in your mindset and mentality can impact greatly to the things that you do. If you think positively about the activities that you do, then you should be able to produce the best result that you can from your work. On the other hand, thinking negatively about your work can make you unmotivated to put in the best effort for it which can result in the lack of quality that you produce.

Work motivation can fluctuate greatly inside of us depending on the mood that we have currently. Have you ever felt like you do not have the motivation to do something that you should do? When you have low motivation, it can feel like you would like to stay away from whatever things that you want to or currently do and you will be much more prone to the urge of procrastination. When you procrastinate, relaxing or do other things which are unrelated to your work in the working hours, that means you waste the time that you should utilize to produce the results that you want from your work and that can only mean bad things if you want to achieve a big success from your work.

Obviously, having a low motivation can impact badly in your productivity too, even if you do not procrastinate. Your mind can be made unfocused during work as you think of other things that you have more motivation about. As a result, even if you do not spend time relaxing or doing other things besides work, you can be liable to the low utilization of the time that you have when you work because of your suboptimal concentration.

It can be easy to fall in the trap of low motivation when you work on something for your success. As is previously described, success most often requires you to do your work for a long time and you can fail or face heavy struggles along the way. It can be hard for you to keep the same motivation along the way especially when you are in a bad situation because of the failure or struggle. Look around and you can see many cases when people give up along the way because they do not have the motivation to continue to work as best as they can and they cannot endure the bad impact from the problems that they meet when they progress in the road to success.

So, what do you need to stay in the line and keep the motivation? You absolutely need a strong mentality and mindset to be able to go all the way to the end results that you want. In the following, Below, I list five things that you need to set your mindset and mentality on so you can have high productivity to achieve success: commitment, resiliency, consistency, desire, and curiosity. I will explain each of them deeper so you know why they are important to do more, better, and faster in your work and you can implement them in your mindset and mentality.

Commitment: The Promise Keeper

One thing that is important for you to have for high productivity is a strong commitment to your work. When you are committed to the work that you do, then you want to do it in a more, better, and faster fashion because you will want to do your work in the best way possible to achieve your goals.

Commitment to work is usually related to the targets that you want to accomplish from your work. The commitment that you have for your work is often the same to how you are attentive to the things that you want from the results of your work. Are you committed to accomplish those results? If you are, then it will be much easier to work on higher productivity because it is correlated with the commitment that you have for your goals. After all, high productivity means that you can progress much faster to achieve the results that you want.

When you work on something, you must try to remember what are the things that you want to produce from the process and whether that something is important to you. If it is not that important to you, then it might be the time to change your objective or change the work that you do because the lower commitment that you have that is caused by the insignificant importance means that you will be more prone to do your work with low productivity or even abandon it completely. The work commitment that you have can support you strongly to have the motivation that you need to do your best work.

Therefore, it is very important that you commit to something that you think will be worthwhile for you. Because of the taxing work that is usually required to achieve big targets, you have to hold your commitment to the things that you really want. Hence, when you decide to start working on something, you must make sure that the achievement of it is the event that you will celebrate and be very happy about. After all, what is the use of your commitment if you do something that you will not like when you get the results? You must think about what are the long-term goals that you have in your work and how are you committed to the work that you need to do for them if you meet some struggles along the way.

If you are seriously committed to the cause of having those goals realized, then it should be a breeze for you to work on it and try to achieve it as soon as possible by having the best productivity from working on it with the Do More Better Faster approach.

Resiliency: The Bouncing Performer

This one is, of course, related to the failures or problems that you may meet during your work. As with all people, all the things that you do at work cannot be always smooth and there might be some times when you fail or meet a big problem that you need to solve to get the results that you want. The bad situation that these kinds of events cause can make you lose the motivation to fill your time with the work you need to do, let alone make the work as productive as possible. It can be hard for you to get back up again as you feel unconfident with yourself because of the work problems that you have met and it can accumulate with the more problems that you experience along the way.

When you meet this bad situation, it is important to be able to get back up again and face the reality by working as good and as fast as possible to not let the situation make you down. For too long. This is what resiliency for. You must also put in the effort to find a way so that the situation can be overcome and you can go back faster to your success progress. Do not lose the motivation to work so you can use the failure as the stepping stone that you need to get the results that you want eventually.

If you put in the effort to overturn the bad situation that you meet during your work, then it might be the case of the high productivity that you need so you can get back up again as soon as possible. After all, high productivity means that you do something more, faster, and better and that kind of support should have a crucial role to make you spend minimum time dwelling with the problems that you have.

Thus, looking at the fact above, resiliency seems to be strongly correlated with the productivity that can be gained from doing your work more, better, and faster. It is joined by the fact that you need to do some work to get back from the failures or other problems that you have at work and the thing that can make the work results great in a shorter time is the productivity that you have. When you can work faster to get out of the problems, then it will be quicker for you too to get the solution that you need to solve them.

The resiliency that you have will provide the base that you need to work productively in the aftermath of the struggles that you face. The struggles that you need to experience might be many, especially if you are serious in chasing success, and the only way to keep getting through them while keep progressing to the results that you want is by having a strong resiliency to work productively despite the bad situation that you may have.

Consistency: The Relentless Pursuer
When you need to work for something in a long time like in the case when you do your work to achieve success or when you do a daily job that you need to do to secure your main income stream, it is important to have a high work consistency to keep working with great intensity in a long period. Only by having work consistency that you will produce the best work results that you can every time and achieve the success that you want from your work.

Work consistency that you should have by always doing your job in your best capacity might be hard to achieve after you have been in some time on your job. When you start, it might be the case of still having a high level of motivation as you set out to accomplish the things that you want from your work. You are still very eager to work your best. You think about the achievement that you can get from your work and predict that it will not take a long time before you are able to see at least some results of your work. However, as the time goes by, you meet with some problems, and your chase to the results that you want seem have not made you any closer to them. Because of this, you might lose your work consistency bit by bit before going down to the path of low productivity work. Of course, it will have a bad impact on the things that you want to accomplish as the low productivity work and the low drive that you have to work in your best capacity make it much longer for you to get the end results. It can even make you stop completely to do your work because you think that the work that you have done has no to little effect on the realization of end goals that you want to realize.

Therefore, you should have it in your mindset that you will not stop working and giving your best in your work until you accomplish the things that you want no matter how long it may seem for you to have to do it. Most of the things that you think are prevention for you to work your best can be solved eventually by using consistent hard work and the productive one of it should make it faster and easier for you. Consistency is a very important thing to maintain until you reach the things that you want at work.

By having a high level of consistency in the work that you do, it should make you be able to improve bit by bit too so you can be more productive and produce better results as time goes by. As being told earlier, the experience that you accumulate from your work can help you in doing things better with a more powerful approach that should be refined as time goes by. Work consistency can help you to improve productivity by learning from the experience that you have had, as long as you still have the drive to keep on pushing on your work.

Desire: The Obsessive Taker

How bad do you want something as a result of your work? That power of desire that you have for that result can be one of the crucial keys to keep on being in a high productivity state when it comes to your work.

When you want something that badly that it borders on being an obsession for you, that means you are willing to go the extra miles and put in the most optimum effort so you can get what you want as soon as possible. Having that kind of desire is in line with what productivity can give to you which Do More Better Faster kind of approach has to offer. High productivity in work should always mean that you can accomplish the works that are needed to achieve your success. The desire that you have for it should make you desire high productive work too.

If you have a high desire for the results that you want, then you should also be willing to spend some extra time to work for it. Combine this fact with the productivity that you have, then it will impact greatly to the success progress that you have. It is because the many hours that you put in for your work, including the extra time, can be utilized optimally by the high productivity of your work.

Having a strong desire also means that you can overcome the urge of procrastination that might come during your work. This is the thing that also can hinder your productivity. It is sometimes hard to not give in when you feel bored and tired of the work that you do. However, as long as you have a strong desire to get the optimum results that you want from your work, then you will want to optimize every opportunity that you have to be able to gain them as much as possible.

When you look at the stories of successful people, it can be made the case that all of them want their success more than anyone else so they can accomplish their achievements at the end. The journey to success often takes a lot of time from the period when the people who are on this journey start until the point when the success has been procured. Now, how many times they might question themselves just like everyone else when the success that they want have not been attained? Maybe much too but in the end, they keep on going because the desire that they have is that strong to achieve the results that they want. Eventually, the results for this strong desire is evident.

The desire that you have at work should be able to help you try to work productively by doing your work more, better, and faster. It is because what your desire wants can be supported to be satisfied significantly by having a highly productive work runs its course for you.

Curiosity: The Reflective Implementer

When you do some work in which you want to gain some results, you might be curious about the most reliable way to be able to accomplish the results that you want as fast and as good as possible. This curiosity trait is the thing that can make you always want to improve yourself to be better for your work. One of the things that must be looked at when you are curious about getting the best work results is the level of productivity that you can have in it.

High productivity means that you can do your work in a better and faster way while accomplishing more. When you are curious about the ways to improve your work, you can take a look further on how you can enhance your productivity to the next level. The approach to do things more, better, and faster might be the thing that you need for that.

Curiosity can also lead you to the urge to find the most updated knowledge and skills related to your work which should be in line with the productive approach of your work. When you have this kind of knowledge and skills and always eager to try to implement them in your work just to see whether they work for you and they can bring you a better work result, then you should be able to continuously improve the work results that you have too. As the world constantly offers new things that can fit your way of work, that means the improvement that you have should be constant too and that can make it an advantage for you in terms of work productivity.

This should mean that you will also try to implement the work approach which is being offered here and try to see the results for yourself. The ones that are proven to make you able to work on more things with better and faster results should be something that you make a habit of as you try to perfect your work. This should be the approach that you need to take to get the optimum advantage of the suggestions that will be given in the next chapters.

The curiosity that you have should also help you when you meet problems in your work besides the resiliency that you have. The curiosity here means that you will want to know how to solve the problems that you have in work so they can be overcome quickly. That in turn will also make you want to know how to do your work better in the future so that you do not have to experience the same failure event again.

So, you have known how to set your mindset and mentality to be able to do the approach of Do More Better Faster optimally. Try to have the five aspects when you want to have the best work results so you can have a high chance to actually produce them.

In the next chapters, we will take a look at what are the things that we can do for highly productive work. The Do More Better Faster approach will be divided into four areas which are:

- Do : The work approaches so you do not delay or abandon your work at the working hours
- More : The work approaches so you can finish more work in the same period
- Better : The work approaches so you can work only on the things that matter
- Faster : The work approaches so you can do things faster

These four areas are divided like that so they can be optimized to improve significantly the four important areas that contributes to the overall level of productivity that you have in your work. By doing the suggestions that are given in each area, you should be able to work optimally in the working hours of yours by resisting the desire to do unproductive things for a significant amount of time and making your work much more effective and efficient.

From the Do More Better Faster, we will begin by discussing the Do approach, the part which handles about the motivation of doing your work, first in the next chapter.

DO: NO MORE WORK EXCUSES

The first from the Do More Better Faster approach is the Do approach. This is the approach that is meant to help you in resisting the urge of using your working hours significantly to do other things that are not related to your work. This is important as we often let ourselves get taken by the desire to relax or do other fun things unrelated to our work.

When we work in our working hours then what are the things that usually happen and distract our work? Can you truthfully say that you spend all the working hours that you have only for work? Granted, it is very rare that people can utilize 100% of the working hours that they have solely for work. Often, we spend a part of them doing other things that we might call "refreshing" ourselves from the stress that we have during our work.

The desire to do unrelated activities to our work can come from many different sources. Maybe it comes from the social media as we want to look at to see some updates in it from time to time, the news website that we keep on scrolling to read the latest info that happens around us, or our co-workers that get us having a conversation about some gossips regarding hot issues that happen recently in the office. Often, we think that it is only a short break from our work and it will take only a few minutes to do the activities. However, usually, we keep going and going and, in the end, we might have spent half to one hour easily without noticing at those activities. If you want to be seriously productive in your work, then you should pay attention to these kinds of things and try to eliminate the ones that do take quite a large portion of your time as they can cut your working hours significantly without even noticing. The lack of true working hours that you spend on your tasks can also make you more stressed as you have to deal with the shorter time that you have for them with their deadlines may come soon. There might be a lower quality of work results because of that.

If we want to talk about high productivity, then the starting point of every productivity, after all, is that you must *do* the work first. Without doing the work, then what is the thing that productivity should optimize for you? Before you move on to the other things in the Do More Better Faster approach, it will be great if you can utilize the working hours that you have mostly for your work. The first problem that you must tackle in your effort for highly productive work, it seems, is to make sure that you have done actual work during the time when you are supposed to do it.

When we talk about truly doing the work that we need to do or not doing it at all during the portion of our working hours, you might think that this is related to the strength of the desire to procrastinate that we have and it is quite true. Looking at the data, it seems that procrastination has become a major problem among us who need to spend time working. Pies Steel, a human resources professor at the University of Calgary's Haskayne School of Business, said that 95% of the population procrastinates at times with 20% has a chronic procrastination problem. This means that most of us have some level of procrastination problem in our work. If we can optimize that time that we use to procrastinate for the work that we do, then it should be a great early point for the high level of productivity that we want in our work.

However, it is very understandable that a person should feel more inclined towards doing other activities unrelated to work. It is because other activities have much less stress and frustration while we usually also feel much happier when we do the things that we enjoy more. In the short term, it is obviously more interesting to do the things that we find fun and enjoyable rather than the work that we need to do because works are what usually make us need to think hard so we can get them done. However, if we think about the things that we want to achieve in the long term, then work is something essential that we have to consistently do.

And it seems that in regard to the things that happen to them, people heavily prefer short-term results than the long-term ones. As Harvard Psychology Professor, Daniel Gilbert, stated, human brains are much more responsive to an immediate threat and not so good at the distant future problems. Moreover, when we think about it, the results of our work can seem to be uncertain and we do not know for sure that whether the things that we do in our work can give the results that we want in the end. All of these can result in the preference that we have towards the activities outside of our work. We prefer the things that can be enjoyed immediately and more certain rather than possibly a much bigger reward that we are not sure whether we are going to get it.

However, although it is hard, we must make sure that we have a high motivation to work hard consistently to achieve what we want. Because the things that we want are what usually matter the most in our life and the only way to get them is through hard work. Whatever the things that we have to do, we need to make sure that we can do them so we always have a chance to get the things that we desire in the end.

The Do from the Do More Better Faster approach is meant to be the opening gate for you to the high productivity that you chase. It is the thing that should keep your resolve to work high so you can really spend your working hours mostly for working.

As the way to apply the Do approach, this book has some suggestions that you can implement regarding that:

- Formulate the catalyst cause
- Step away from the distractor
- Split the working hours from the others
- Optimize work context
- Get someone to watch you

As we want to learn how to create a highly productive work by understanding this Do approach, we will take a deeper look at the first suggestion in the next chapter.

DO 1: FORMULATE THE CATALYST CAUSE

When you think about the definition of your success as you may have done in the previous chapter, you might want to reflect whether it has a strong correlation with you and it is a thing that you seriously want in life. Because by doing that, it should make sure that you have got the optimum motivation to work when it comes to the cause that you have to do it.

If you want to aim for high productivity in your work, then you might want to ask yourself this question: what is the end result that I want to achieve from my work so I need to put in highly productive work? The answer to that question can be the important thing that gives you the drive to do your work and keep on trying to optimize the working hours that you have. It is because the reason for your work is why you do any work at all. The why always precedes the how on the things that you do.

Think about an example of a reward that is offered to you when you do some kind of work. When one reward offers you more money for more or less the same workload compared to another offer that gives you less money for a more or less similar task, which one that you will do? It is no brainer that you will choose the first work with more rewards. The strength of the targets that you want to achieve when you want to do your work is important so you can dismiss other options that you have in the working hours, including relaxing or do other things that are unrelated to your work, without having to think hard about it.

You should pick the cause that is strong for you so you can have enough motivation to do your work. Now, what should you do to make sure that you formulate a strong cause? First of all, you must make sure that the targets that you have resonate with the aspects that you think are important in life. Do you prefer to have a social impact in your life, a financial condition that is great, or probably the influence that you can have from yourself? Be truthful about it and set the cause that you want at your work according to this. The more the work goals that you have resonate with the aspect that you regard as important in your life, the more strength that it should have to motivate you to prioritize work in your working hours.

Besides the important aspects that you have in life, you might want to consider some other things to do when you want to strengthen the cause that you have in work:

- **Evaluate the positive impact that the goals can have for the people who are close to you**. Often, the things that matter the most to you is not only yourself but the people who you love. These people can be the members of your family or other people who you care about their well-being. Reflecting on what is the level of positive effects that the goals might have to those people around you can be one important way to measure whether they can be something that can seriously motivate you to work or not
- **Think about the success that you most celebrate in the past**. You may have looked to the success that other people did and think that is the kind of achievement that you aspire for yourself to accomplish in the future. Take a look at the success that you have celebrated mostly in the past and make you feel most impressed about. Consider that as the things that you want to get from your work
- **Bring deadlines to the goals that you have set**. After you have formulated the goals that you need to

achieve in your work then it will be better if you have a target of when those goals need to be achieved. That way, you should feel more motivated to put in the work because you have a clear time definition of when you should be able to get the results that you want from your work

- **Be realistic**. This point is strongly correlated to the deadline that you have set yourself for the success that you want to achieve. It is great if you can achieve a very big goal from your work in a very short time. But often it is not good to put that kind of condition as your targets because unrealistic targets might have the opposite effect on your work motivation. You might think that it is impossible to achieve your targets no matter how hard the work that you do for them. Therefore, it is important to add a realistic point of view to it and consider the ideal time that you need to accomplish the goals from your current condition. Of course, you must try to achieve them as fast as you can later as it is even better if you can exceed the deadlines that you have set

- **Set gradual targets and milestones**. The big targets that you want to achieve might not be accomplished in a short time. Therefore, in the meantime, it is important to set some mini targets which relate themselves strongly with the big targets that you want to achieve but smaller in scale and easier to accomplish. If the eventual success that you want to achieve has a deadline in years then the gradual targets should be set in months, weeks, or even days. By having them, you can be sure to stay motivated even when you still have not reached your grand goals while also tracking the progress of your work related to that success.

If you follow the suggestions as being told above, then it should be much easier for you to create some causes for your work that are strong and motivate you significantly to work. That way, you should think twice when you want to abandon your work in the working hours because doing so might make it longer for you to accomplish the things that you really want in your life.

DO 2: STAY AWAY FROM THE DISTRACTOR

This suggestion for the Do approach should be pretty logical in terms of its relation to optimize your time to actually work. As has been told previously in this book, the work that we do is often distracted by things unrelated to it. Those things can make us spend a major portion of our working hours doing other activities besides work. So, what should we do if we want to be serious in accomplishing our work and avoid the distractions that can be met during our working hours? Of course, you should try your best to stay away from those distractions!

This means that you should try to do anything necessary for that purpose. Limit or even cut completely the access that you have to the distractions if they bother you too much or try to place yourself far from it when you need to be highly productive in your work. If you often get distracted by the update notifications on your social media or by the games that you have in your gadget, then you must be able to restrict yourself so you never put on your hands on the gadget that brings the distractions unless it is for an urgent matter like reply messages related to your work or see something which is needed to complete your job. Or if you really need high productivity in doing your current work, then you should put your gadget somewhere safe where it is hard for you to access it during the work. If you often feel the urge to join the discussions that your colleagues have in the desk not too far from you, then you should seriously promise yourself that you only join in for a short amount of time (commit not to be taken away far too long in the conversation) or probably you should delay from having the conversation with them until the break time if the discussion is unrelated to the work that you do.

Well, let's face it. When it comes to something that can make you delay or abandon your work during the working hours, then the distractions that you have can play a seriously major part in it. Thus, to be much more effective in dealing with them, then you should reflect and make a list on what are the things that you think as major distractions during the time that you need to be productive.

These distracting things are probably different from each and every one of us. For example, someone might be distracted the most by the social medias that he has his account on because he is usually very active in it while another person might not be too distracted by the social media because she does not have a social media account or she can keep herself from the social media during working hours without too much effort given. It can be important for you to have the list of significant distractions because by having that, we will know for sure what are the things that we need to stay away from especially during the time when we should work seriously. It is so that we can be consistent in utilizing most of the time that we have in the working hours for work and not for the other things which are unrelated to it.

To make the list more comprehensive and can cover most of the significant distractions, when you formulate it, reflect back on the work that you have done until now and think what are the significant things that take away a major part of your working hours besides work. Put them in the list and keep it as an open list that you can keep on updating every time when you find other things that cause a significant enough distraction for you in your work. Note that when you try to list the distractions, those things should be something that seriously are major distractions for you at work. Something that you only do probably five to ten minutes a day besides work should not do too much harm in the high productivity that you want to achieve. When you think of some things that can take more than half an hour each when you do your work activities in a day, then they are most probably the things that you must put in on your list so you can keep away from them during work.

Try to keep the list somewhere that you can see during your work so you can keep being reminded of the things that you should delay first when you work. This is important especially in the condition when you have a deadline which is already near for some of your works. When you disregard the list or completely forget to avoid the significant distractions, you might put yourself to difficulty and more stress that is not necessary because you keep on giving in to the distractions that you have during work. The completion of your work and the quality that you produce from it can be given a bad impact because you do other activities unrelated to your work significantly during the working hours. Remember that you can those things in a significant amount of time after you have done your work in the working hours. You can think about it as a reward that you can get when you have optimized your working hours mostly for the work that you need to do. Be patient and keep the commitment to work when you are still in the period when you have to work. That is the important part of the mindset to have when you seriously want to work in high productivity.

Distractions can keep appearing anywhere at any point during our work. Only by trying actively to stay away from it and having the mindset to optimally utilize the time that you have in the working hours, you can keep yourself in the motion needed to do all of your work.

DO 3: SPLIT THE WORKING HOURS FROM THE OTHERS

Another thing that you can do regarding the optimization of your working hours is to define a clear limit between the time when you need to work and the time when you can do other things that are unrelated to it. This is important so you can improve the commitment that you have for work significantly during the time when you need to do it, especially if you are someone who works for yourself or you are a person who can work according to the schedule that you set yourself. It can be important too for the employee as the working hours that you have might be not too rigid. There can be the day as an employee when you need to do overtime to finish your work or are able to accomplish what you need to do early. It is important too to set the allocation of the hours in the day firmly in your mind when you have not done so as it can improve your productivity in the hours dedicated to your work.

You might ask, why it is so important to set the division for yourself on the working hours and the other activities hours when you want to work more freely? Probably you are the type of person who likes the fact when you can determine the time when you rest and when you work as the day goes. What is the harm if you do something like that? Well, it is because, as a human, we can be more committed to something that is certain rather than the uncertain one in our minds.

Research done in Britain has conducted an experiment about this. They set an experiment where some of the participants in the experiment who are being told that they are certain to receive a painful shock and the others are being told that they have a 50% chance to receive it. The conclusion that comes out from the experiment says that the research participants who know for sure that they are going to get a painful shock are calmer and less agitated compared to their peers who are told that they have a 50% chance of getting the shock. It seems that certainty can make you feel more secure. After all, there is a logic to it when we think about it. If we know that something is certain, then we will be able to plan for the things that we need to do and prepare for it in a more precise way. If we do not know something for sure, then there will be a doubt in our mind whether we need to do something optimally to anticipate it if that thing happens or we should put in the effort if that thing does not happen. There can be half-hearted efforts for the thing that we should do between the two choices of action.

Therefore, it will be good if you can draw the line of certainty between the working hours that you have from the time when you can do other activities. Your mind can be more easily controlled that way and can be more resistant to the urge to procrastinate because it knows the certainty of having some other time in the day to do the relaxing activities. You can also think beforehand about what are the things that you can accomplish in the work that you do that day if you know the approximate hours when you can do the work. Thus, you are able to make sure whether some things in the work probably need more focus from you on that day compared to the others in terms of the productivity that you want and the time that you have for your work.

When you allocate the time that you have in a day for working activities and other activities, then it should not be too much trouble for you most probably because most of us already have some kind of standard habit in a day on when you start working and when you finish working. You need to make sure, though, that you have already optimized the allocation of time that you have in a day for work and allocate the time as you need for the other things. You may also need to evaluate for a bit before you begin each day on how much time you can allocate for work the next day. There might be some particular days when you need to allocate more working hours than usual because there are some works that need to be done fast and there might be other days when you need to allocate fewer working hours because there are some personal matters that you need to attend to. The important thing to remember is to always know your prioritization and optimize the time that you have as appropriate for the things that you need to do on that day.

This approach can be very important if you are an employee who wants to do some side business to achieve success. As we know, the priority when you are still an employee should be the work that you have to do for your company. However, the hours before or after it might be good to be allocated for building your side business. Make sure, though, that you have already allocated enough time for the work that you have to do as an employee so that you can keep accomplishing your main job well even when you do a side business. Do not ever run the side business in the working hours when you need to do your job as an employee as that means you are not respectful to the job that gives you the main income you need while you keep continuing to build your side business. Allocate the time to do it only when you have finished what you are supposed to finish for your employee's works that day.

Setting a clear definition between working and other hours is an important suggestion for this Do approach because of the phycological advantage that it can give you for the resolution of doing your job in the time when you are supposed to do it. After there is the certainty that you formulate for yourself, you just need to commit to do it.

DO 4: OPTIMIZE WORK CONTEXT

The things around your work environment can sometimes be an important factor to improve the work motivation that you have in your working hours. The preferred work context where you are in during the period when you need to do your work can be one of the crucial things that make you more committed to doing your work.

Imagine if you work in a place where you feel uncomfortable in doing so and in the time when you feel you should do other things than work. How will that affect the work resolve that you may have? A much easier defection to other activities unrelated to work might be in line for you because you might not stand the frustration working in the work environment that you do not like.

Therefore, it is important to prepare the work environment that you prefer as optimal as possible. Set some time for yourself to think about what kind of work environment that you prefer and seem to be able to get the best out of you in regards to the work process that you do. After you have defined it, then it is time to implement your definition so you can try working in the preferred work environment the next time when you need to work.

Work context can come in the form of your preferred place, time, and facilities around you that you want to use to work. You might want to think about them in a separate way so you know what kind of settings that you want for your work in each of them. You can reflect in the past and see the period when it seems that the work environment can optimize the motivation that you have for work. What kind of things that shape the work context for you during that time? Keep it in your mind so you can consider it when you think and implement your optimal work environment.

Another thing that you can consider when you define the preference is your personality. In fact, this might heavily influence your preference. You need to ask yourself: what kind of personality do you have? Are you the person who prefers working where and when there is a lot of people or you prefer a quiet place where you can concentrate more on the things that you do? Are you the person who is creative or more to the analytical type? Considering the traits that you have can define what kind of work environment that you prefer if you are confused about it. If you like to work with a lot of people around you, then consider the place and time when you can do that and implement otherwise if you prefer the quiet place. Be considerate about the situation where you feel the most comfortable to work then use it to formulate your optimal work environment.

After you have defined the place, time, and facilities that you need to work optimally, you need to consider the possibility that is attributed to the procurement of them for your work. If you work as an employee, probably your office has some restrictions regarding the place and time that you can work on. Try as best as you can to get the preferred work environment where you can work optimally. If it is possible and you are comfortable to do it, then maybe you can, for example, try to work some of your office jobs at home if you have the preference of doing it in your home environment in the time when you are already outside of your office hours. That way, you can have much less workload when you need to go to the office and the results of your work should be better. Probably you need to talk to the people who are responsible for your workplace and time, such as your supervisor, to show them that your work results can be more productive if you do them in the work environment that you prefer. If they see that your argument makes sense and can bring advantages to the company, then they will have a strong reason to let you work in your preferred work environment. This might not be needed when you work for your own business or your office has a flexible requirement for the employees' work condition as you are much freer to decide what kind of context where you will work in.

It is also important to consider the budget that you have in terms of providing the optimal work environment if you have not got the right resources to immediately set. You need to buy some and it can come from your personal financing.

It is nice if you can have the best of everything in your preferred work environment but it might not be realistic in terms of the budget that you have currently. Do some concessions and buy the things that can make you much closer to the work environment that you prefer in the budget that you have. When you have got the budget to buy the things that can provide you with the best work environment later, then you can upgrade your work context to be as good as it can be for you.

Think about the work environment in terms of place, time, and facility that can bring the most motivation from you to work so you will not use it as a reason to procrastinate. This does not mean you cannot work outside the ideal work environment but it will be much better if you can as the means to give you additional drive to do your work. You might also want to allocate the working hours that you have in the day to fit with the time that you prefer to work so this aspect can also be more optimized. But, of course, you must allocate the working hours not just in the time that you prefer to work as you might not be able to finish your work by using that time only. Optimize your work environment to support your work motivation as well as you can but prioritize the work that you need to do to accomplish it well.

DO 5: GET SOMEONE TO WATCH YOU (REALLY)

Really? Really.

Well, to be clear, this does not mean that you have to get someone acting like a stalker and watching every little thing that you do during your workday. You do not have to ask a person to always be there near you in all of your working hours to make sure that you do the things that you are meant to do in that period. Probably there will not be someone who is in the right mind likes to do that anyway for a person.

But the point here is you might need someone who can see the progress that you have done in your work and give constructive feedback regarding the things that you did and the results that you have produced in the process. The discussion for the progress might be periodical, like in monthly regularity. The main objective of the discussion being held is to keep you responsible for the things that you need to do as it will not look good for you if you say that you only have no to little progress during your discussion because you do not optimize the time that you have for work. By having someone with whom you can talk about the things that you have done at work, then you can be more motivated to work optimally because you want to show that person that you can do it. You can also get some constructive feedback along the way which may do some good to the improvement of your work.

The suggested things that you need to discuss is your work progress, results, and what have you done in the period before the discussion takes place to optimize yourself in your work. Discuss also the things that seem to halt you to work significantly and what can be done about it. It might be better to set and note some targets too that are wanted to be attained in your work before the discussion begins. This is so you can also measure your work against them too during the discussion.

When you want to ask someone to do the discussion with you, you have to be sure that person is someone that you can trust and can give you the feedback that you need to keep improving the approach that you have at work. It might be your spouse, friend, or someone that you regard as a mentor. The discussion that takes place periodically does not have to be done face to face if you or the person that you ask to "watch over you" do not have the time for that. It can be using the media like a video call or even messaging application if you must. The most important thing if you want to do this is to be disciplined in doing the discussion on the period that you have the agreement on so the discussion can produce many benefits from it.

If you plan to do the discussion with someone like your spouse or your friend, then probably the person can also be watched over by you too if the person wants it by he/she tells you too about the progress that he/she has made in work so you both can get the optimum benefit from the discussion. You can ask more than one person to discuss the work progress too so there are more people who can give feedback and more people can benefit from the discussion. If it is someone that you think as a mentor in your work, then besides telling the person about your progress, you can emphasize valuable advice on some aspects that he/she can give to you because a mentor most probably has more knowledge, skills, and experience than you in the work. Try not to take it to the heart if there are some criticisms during the discussion that you conduct but instead, be appreciative of it as that person tries to help you in making your work process better. Be open and reflect on the feedback as something that you can make the base of your improvement in work from including improving the implementation of the Do approach for your productivity.

If you need to and the discussion about your work seems to have some things that are better not to be known by other people, then you can ask the person to keep the matter that is being discussed as confidential. For that purpose, discuss with only the people that you can trust to keep the discussion a secret. You do not want for the discussion activity to instead make you feel down because the things that are being discussed are known by other people who are not supposed to notice about it.

Regarding the period when you want to discuss the work progress, set some period which seems friendly to you and the person that you ask to do the discussion with. Probably the preference of the time is more heavily preferred to the desire of the person that you ask to discuss with as you are the one who initiates it and has more stakes in the discussion. Do it in the period which is not too hectic with a probably monthly period as a minimum. That way you can have more matters to discuss too and the pattern of your work process is more visible to be discussed and be improved on during the discussion.

Before the time that you want to conduct the discussion, it might be better also to prepare what you want to share in the process. Being prepared in everything is much better than if you are not. This does not mean that you use the time when you prepare to make up your work progress as being truthful in the discussion regarding the progress and the results that you get should be the way to get optimal benefit from the discussion. Instead, you can use the preparation time to think about what are the things that you want to ask and discuss to improve your work approach in the time after the discussion is done. That way, you can optimize the discussion process for the exact improvement that you want in your work.

MORE: NO MORE UNOPTIMIZED EFFORT

After we have looked at the ways to optimize the first part from the Do More Better Faster approach to improve your productivity, which is especially formulated to trigger your motivation to work significantly, now is the time to move to the second part of the approach which is More. This is the concept where we should do things as much as possible in the time that we have during our working days without having to compromise the resulting quality of the work results.

Time is a limited resource as there are only 24 hours in a day for each of us. What we do and finish in our work during those hours determines how fast we can achieve the result that we want. That means if we can do and finish more work in the same period, then it should be faster for us too to get the results that we want. The important thing for our work productivity on this More part is how to find and implement some ways so we can complete more workload at the same time that we have in a day.

After all, all of us want to succeed as soon as possible, right? If it is true that success is something that you can achieve by accumulating the workloads that are needed to be done as the requirement for it, then it will be much better for you if you can accumulate them in the shortest time possible. That way, you should be able to enjoy your achievements much sooner. One way that objective can be gained is by doing as much as possible in the working hours that we have so we can accumulate the required workload for the success fast. Doing so will also logically boost your productivity as you can accomplish more in the same time.

However, if we have the wrong approach, then try to do more work at the same time can have its drawback in terms of the goodness of the results that we can produce during the working time. We might compromise quality as a result of trying to get more done at the same time if we are not careful in the approach that we have regarding the work. When you try to see what kind of approach that you need to do so you can do more things at the same period without sacrificing the work results, then you need to consider about the targets that you want to accomplish from those works of yours and what are the ways that they can be synchronized with other works' targets so no work will be done badly because we do not watch over the results that must be produced by those works. This can be done if you are selective with what kind of work approach that you implement to do that. Remember that bad work quality can also mean that you need to redo the majority of your work all over again because people who are affected by the results of the work that you do might be deeply unsatisfied with it. That means that it can make you take a longer time because you have to revise your work in a major way.

So, the thinking is: What are more works that you can do in the same period so more workloads can be accomplished in that same period compared to before? What are the things that you can do so you can keep on maintaining or even improving the quality of the work results when you do those works on the same period? Those are the questions that you should answer when you want to do this More approach. Doing more things without compromising their quality should be the mindset that you set on yourself if you want to seriously produce results with high productivity. An optimal effort with the time that you have should be the thing that you chase during your work.

This approach of More means that you cannot leave important things unworked for if you have the time and chance to do it. It means that you do whatever you can to ensure that you have used the time that you have in your working hours to accomplish most tasks that you have. You have to make sure that whatever the things that you do in your work, they have to contribute to the completion of your workloads in the most efficient way. If you have done your work for some times, then you might need to reflect on whether the time that you have spent in your work has been optimized for completing most of your workloads and whether that period has given much in terms of the things that you want to produce from your work process. Some improvements might be needed to ensure that you can do more work in the same period and some work habits might need to be upgraded or replaced by better habits so you can do more on the same working day after this reflection has been done.

Hence, in trying to apply more of this More approach, what are the things that you can do in your work so you can do more in the same period? These are some suggestions for you to do that will be discussed deeper in the next chapters:

- Applying the right to-do list that you can take correct action from
- Take care of the long-term works during your working hours
- Group the same kind of tasks to be worked at the same time
- Delegate selective tasks to the appropriate people
- Dismiss the micromanagement which is avoidable

All of these suggestions can be implemented so you can achieve more with the same duration of your work. We will talk more about each of them so you can have a better understanding of them and can implement them correctly in the work that you do. We will start with the first one which is related to the correct implementation of the popular tool, the to-do list.

MORE 1: APPLY THE RIGHT TO-DO LIST

As has been described in the previous chapter about the importance of cause for your productivity to do any work, it seems that it is pretty important for people to have targets that they can look on so they know why they have to do the work before they can trigger the motivation to do it. When you do your work daily, it is better for you too to have some kind of targets that you have to accomplish on that day so you try to achieve more in the same working day.

The targets can come in the form of a to-do list that you have made for that working day. The list usually consists of the things that you must accomplish during that day so you can consider yourself as highly productive. This list is a good thing to have for supporting the More approach in your work because of the way that it can give you some guidance to work more in the same period.

When you have planned about the things that you want to do in a day, you can optimize the amount of work that you do because you can think more clearly in terms of the activities that you have to do in that day and the results that you want to achieve too. If you think about it when you already work during that day, then there might be something that you miss or something important which you forget to do because of the lack of planning beforehand. Therefore, set a little time just before your working day or in the morning before you begin your work on that day to set the optimal to-do list for you. Think about the things that you can do with the hours that you have on that day and what are the works that you can do to optimize your time to be highly productive. When you create your to-do list, you must think about the urgency of the works too. List the important things that have a shorter deadline for you first before doing the listing on the other tasks. That way, you can have a to-do list which should help you to organize the best kinds of works that you have to do too on that day.

The success that you want to target from your work should also be a part of the consideration for you to make your to-do list. Think about the big and gradual targets that you want to achieve and how the works that you list can support you to do that. The to-do list which is formulated can help you to accomplish the works that can bring you to progress faster too in the success that you want. This is important because you may lose sight of your intended goals if you do not spend time planning your works to get you closer to realizing them.

Besides the things that have already been stated, here are some other things that you might want to do so you can create a right to-do list that can serve as significant support in your More approach:

- **Make the things in your to-do list precise**. When you formulate the things that you should do in work, you can be susceptible of making them abstract and do not have a clear definition when people first look at them. Try your best to make the points in your to-do list precise, measurable, and simple so you do not confuse yourself when you need to look at them in your workday.
- **Take a note for them somewhere you can look easily**. Your to-do list is meant to be formulated as a guide for you to optimize the time that you have with as many work activities as possible. Therefore, it is much better if you take a note for it somewhere when you formulate it and keep the notes somewhere close so you can go back to it again when you need direction on what you need to finish that day.

- **Be aggressive but realistic when planning the things**. The main objective of your to-do list is to help you do more work on a working day so you must treat it as such when you formulate it. Be aggressive in condensing the things that you want to do but keep the realistic point of view as too many activities that cannot be done in a day might actually have a bad effect for your work motivation.

- **Allocate enough time to formulate it and be disciplined**. As it can be something important to guide you in going through your workday, then you should give some special attention to your to-do list even if it is just for a short time. Allocate 15-30 minutes to create your to-do list and make it a habit in your day to do it so you can consistently use the tool as your way to optimizing the work that you do.

- **Reflect on the past to-do list that you have done, watch the implementation, and improve**. If you have made it a habit to formulate a to-do list for your working days, then you should have accumulated some experience on the tool application and how you implement them. Evaluate on the formulation and implementation that you have done in the past and make your next to-do list with the consideration of the evaluation results as there might be some things that you can improve when you try to look closer at this.

The most important thing that you have to remember when using the to-do list tool for your More approach is the commitment to implement what you have formulated in the list. There can be some laziness after you have created the to-do list with some aggressiveness as you think that it will be quite a workload for you to do all of the things listed. Be committed and try to see it through the to-do list by completing as many items as possible during your working hours. From there, it is a matter of evaluation and improvement to see what are the things that you can do better when you formulate your next to-do lists.

MORE 2: TAKE CARE OF THE LONG-TERM ONES

When you do your work and have completed the jobs that you are supposed to do in the day, the jobs that have near deadlines in them, on a much earlier time before the working hours in the day finish, you might be tempted to take a break and just relax for the rest of the day as you feel that you have not got anymore job that you should finish. When it can be the case of taking it easier during the rest of the day as the deadline pressure is much less for the work that you need to do at the moment, you should consider using that extra time that you have to do some other work activities that seem to still have a long deadline. The reason is that by doing that, you can relieve yourself from some deadline pressure in the future while maintaining high productivity in the entire working hours that you have. This kind of approach doing your work is in line to the More concept which says that you should try to utilize your working hours to accomplish more workload whenever it is possible.

You might indeed sacrifice some short-term happiness that you can have by enjoying the rest of the working hours that you have. After all, you can legitimately use the extra time to do some relaxing activities or play with your social media account. However. if you think about it, working on some long-term commitments in your work can bring many benefits for you. First thing is, of course, the calmness that you have when working on the tasks. By knowing the work that you do still have a long time before its deadline, your mind can think much more clearly to produce the best result for your work. You might even be able to do the work faster with better results because of this much less pressure. Moreover, you can also recheck some of the work's important details a few times before you submit the work to the people who you are responsible for.

Besides, you might not know whether you actually have enough time to do that work in the future. There might be other works or projects that suddenly come up and they require your immediate attention which means that it can reduce significantly the time that you can use to work on those long-term works in the future. Therefore, to be able to safeguard yourself from that potential trouble and make you calmer to face some sudden urgent tasks, it will benefit you to try to finish a part or even all of them now when you have some extra time available for you.

Working on some long-term commitment works should also progress you much faster to the success that you want from your work. By being able to work quicker on more tasks that are needed for your success, you should be able to get yourself closer to the accomplishments that you want earlier. You can also improve yourself faster by learning quicker from your work with the long-term things that you can finish. They can be seen as the stepping stones that you need to take before you can accomplish the achievements that you want on a shorter period.

If you have run out for the things that you should do which have deadlines on them, then it might be the case of finding out what other works that you can do in the extra period which is in line with the targets that you have in work. For someone who does business, it can be an easy thing to find because there are always works that you can do to make your business closer to the success that you want. If you have done the work that you think you need to do in the short-term or long-term, then to utilize the extra time that you have, you can think of a way to innovate your product/service so it can better serve your customer, try some media that you can use to improve the promotion of your product/service, or probably lookup for a way to streamline your business process. If you are an employee, then you might need to think more about the things that you can do to realize your targets related to the work that you do in the office. Obviously, if you have a side business on your own and think to utilize the time that you have to be productive in it, you need to restrain yourself and must not use the time remaining in your office hours to do that. This is because as an employee, you should respect your role and focus your effort during the office hours for the work that you have to do within your responsibility as an employee.

Then what you should do? Maybe you can try to learn some new skills online which are related to the jobs that you have or maybe you can try to help your co-workers with their project if they need help for something which you can do. There are always things that you can do for your work if you are willing to look up for them.

The most important point related to this suggestion is you should not waste the extra working hours that you have if you seriously want to achieve success in your work and have high productivity. By working on the things that still have long-term deadlines or other things that are related to the targets that you want to realize in your work, you will make sure that you can optimize the time that you have for work even though you might have finished the works that you are supposed to do that day. When you do those extra works on your working hours, think about it as a way to gain yourself some capital that you can use in the future to reach your work targets. That way, you should be more motivated to finish the tasks that you actually still do not have to finish for a while in the extra time that you have got.

MORE 3: GROUP THE SAME KIND OF TASKS TOGETHER

There might be some works that you can do together so you can save up more time to do other things in your working day. To recognize what are the works that you can do together, you should try to analyze the workloads that you have and see whether you can do some of them together in a time sequence to make the process of completing them more streamlined.

For example, you might have to do some tasks related to the report that you have to complete for your supervisor, which are analyzing some data to be used on the creation of your report, writing some narrative on it, and discussing the materials of the report with your colleagues who have some responsibilities for the report too. By batching all of those report related tasks, you should be able to do each of them faster because when you do one of the tasks, you have more possibility to relate the thing that you have done in it to complete the other tasks that are in one grouping. As a result, you can do all the works in one group faster.

The thing that makes the tasks in a group faster to get done is because of the strong relevancy that it has with each other. The connectedness that each of the tasks has means that you can work on the thing that makes them relates to each other at the same time. This fact is important because it also means that the more relevancy that you can find for the tasks that you have in the group, the faster you should be able to work on those tasks at the same period.

Doing the tasks that you have to do in a grouping also has another benefit as it should also help you in the quality of the works that you do. Thus, it can be a two-way benefit for you in terms of productivity. When you work on the same grouping of tasks, your mind should very much focus on the things that are related in those tasks. By making sure that all of them have some relevance to each other, then that focus on the things that make the tasks related should be more amplified to make you produce better work results for them in the time that you work for the grouping. As in the case with the more tasks that you can do at the same time if the relevancy is closer to each other, the quality of your work should logically be better too because of the unseparated focus that you have on them.

When trying to group the same kind of tasks, it might be best to think about those that have the same main task which governs them or the similar media in which you do those tasks in. It can be whatever relevancy which can connect your works but it seems that those two things are the ones which we can find the relevancy in the works that we do the most. After that, it is up to your thinking to see what groupings that you should use to be able to streamline your tasks to produce the most productivity in your work. For example, you may want to group a discussion that you have to do with other colleagues with other discussions that you need to have in your work (media) or you might want to batch it with the main task that it is related to which is a project that you need to accomplish (main task). Either way can be the best as long as you consider what is the kind of grouping that gives you the most benefit to do much more at the same period.

The groupings that you have made concerning your work should also be flexible according to the latest update of tasks that you have to do. There can be some sudden works related to the groupings that you have made or probably the work that you have grouped to do at the same time has lost its urgency to be done because of some events. In a case of something like that, it will be good if you can update the groupings and see whether there is something that needs to be done in its work process because of the immediate changes.

Besides the things that have been mentioned related to the practice of the tasks grouping, here are some other things that you might want to consider:

- **Consider the urgency of the tasks too**. There might be some task members in your grouping that should be done much earlier than the others. Consider this when you try to make the groupings as it might not be a good idea to delay the part of the grouping which is urgent just so you can do it together with the other tasks. Prioritize on doing that task first even if it does not have to be in a grouping so you can deal with the urgency of the task too (or maybe consider working on the grouping in a much earlier time).

- **Try to group as many tasks as possible**. As more tasks that can be grouped are joint together to be worked at the same time in the day, the things that you can do at that period should be more too. Consider all the tasks that you might have and group as many tasks as possible to be worked together so you can get more optimum benefits from the task grouping practice.

- **Remember other tasks too that are not correlated**. When you work on the tasks which are in one group, it can be easy for you to forget the other tasks that you might have to do in the current working day. Remember to see the urgency of other tasks too and do them first if they are important to be finished before the other tasks in your grouping are completed.

Remember that the relevancy of the tasks in the grouping is the key to make you work more tasks at the same time. But you should not forget about the urgency of the tasks that you have in your working day. Thus, you are still able to complete the things that should be done on that day besides the ones in the groupings that you have already made.

MORE 4: DELEGATE SELECTIVE TASKS

Now, the tasks that you think you should do in your working day might be the tasks that can be delegated to someone else so you can achieve more in the same time. The important thing here is to select the tasks that are appropriate to be delegated and, after the delegation is done, focus more on the tasks that are in line with your responsibility.

The reason why you have to delegate tasks when it is proper to do so seems obvious. By having the tasks worked by someone else, you can work on the other things which may require your attention much more. You can accomplish more in the same time by having the works done in parallel on a period. The productivity of your work should improve too because the tasks that you work are the ones that are more suitable for you.

Besides, when you see some of the tasks that have to be completed in the working day, there might be some which are more appropriate if they are given to someone else. It might be the case also that you get the tasks so it can be entrusted from you to someone else who you think is the most appropriate to do the task. The important thing to remember here is to look up at the details of the tasks and do not do the delegation just because you want to relax or do other things unrelated to your work. Instead, to be much more productive and practice the More approach during your delegation activity, you should use the window of time that you get from freeing yourself from the task to do some other things which can be more crucial or appropriate for you to do.

However, you should be selective at the tasks that you want to delegate and when you do it, it is better that you utilize the time that you have yourself to do some other things related to work so you can improve your work productivity because of the delegation. It is important too to remember that you should explain the task to the person that you give the delegation too in a clear and precise way so the person knows what he/she should do regarding the work.

When thinking about the delegation of the tasks that you have, you must also think about the supervisory that you have to do regarding the tasks results that you have entrusted to someone else especially if the tasks are being known by other people to be given to you. It might be better too if you let the related people know that you have delegated the task to other people so that the responsibility can be divided and the person that you delegate your task with will feel much more accountable about it. If the task results are good, then the person who mostly does it should get the reward or praise that he/she deserves too and that also goes for the opposite. When the work is done, you should also check again the results that you get from the person that you do the delegation to and make sure of the quality is good.

The people who you should consider to delegate your tasks can be many. It can be your subordinates or your employees if you have a business, your peers, or even your supervisor. However, it is important that you delegate only the tasks which are fit to be given to each of the group. Here are some suggestions for the tasks that you should think about delegating for them and what you should do regarding the delegation activity for each of the group members:

- **Subordinates/employees**
  When you have some subordinates/employees who work with you, then you should entrust the work that is more tactical and suits their function to them. If the

subordinates/employees that you have are still new, then you might not have the full belief that they can do the job, especially if the job is quite important for the company, as you still do not have any memory about how they do their work. Therefore, if possible, try to give the job that is easier first for the ones who are still new with the harder ones will be given as the subordinates/employees have more experience that is relevant in them.

Supervisory is especially important when you deal with the delegations that you give to your subordinates/employees as the result of their work will be your responsibility too. When you do the supervisory, it is important to keep it in a way that lets them still do all the work in the way which they think is the best while you watch from the side. Give the objectives of the task and the result that you expect from it without too many details on how to do it (just pointers if necessary). Let them ask questions to you if they need it. However, the important thing is you should not be tempted to work the jobs that you delegate yourself as much as possible because it can set a bad precedence in the future. The subordinate/employee will get used to being helped a lot in their work by you and you do not want that because you can never let them work alone while you completely do other things if that is the case. The final goal of the delegation with your subordinates/employees is always to make them able to work the delegated tasks all by themselves and produce a good quality work result while at it. If there happen to be mistakes when you check the work results, then you should let them correct the mistakes while giving some pieces of advice on the expectation.

- **Peers**

  When you try to ask one or more of your peers to complete some tasks, you need to make sure that it is within the responsibility of your peers and you have a good reason to do so. Because, obviously, if you just give them tasks and it seems it is just because you are too lazy to do it, then your peers will not take it kindly and might not want to get the tasks done. Even if they do, then they will not do it seriously. The good reasons can be that you are very full of urgent things on your work at the moment or it is not within your area of responsibility and expertise to do that job.

  If the reason is that you are too full of the urgent tasks that you have to do at the moment, then make sure you delegate only the part of the task that you cannot handle to your peers. When it is done, then give the person your thanks and check again while correcting it yourself if there happen to be some mistakes that you identify. Every person has his/her own business in work and you must be thankful if your peer agrees to help you if the reason for the delegation is not because that the related responsibility of the work. Make sure to explain what you know regarding the task whatever your reason is so the person can do the work right without any confusion to the expectation of the work results.

- **Supervisor**

  If the task that you get from other sources seems to be more appropriate to be done by your supervisor, then you should explain the matters to your supervisor about why he/she should be the one to handle it. It can be because the realm of responsibility of the task is more appropriate to the supervisor level or it needs the kind of experience and mastery which can only be done by your supervisor. Whatever it is, you need to think about it carefully as you do not want to give the task which actually can be done by you.

Another matter is probably that you want your supervisor to assign to another person because you are already too full at the moment or it is not within your responsibility and there is another person in your team who should be more in line with the nature of the work. In that case, talk to your supervisor about it and describe the details of the task so your supervisor can consider the best way to distribute the task based on the info.

As being said at the beginning of this chapter, consider the tasks that you should delegate and the person who is the most appropriate to do them. You do not want to give the wrong task to the wrong person as doing that will make the result of the work not as good as expected.

MORE 5: AVOID TOO MUCH MICRO

Details can be good when you do your work especially if it is related to some tasks of data analysis that you should do. However, having too much attention to your work can be bad for your productivity. If it is some kind of redundant details that you should not give attention to it too much, then it might be the best to just let it go and use the time to do other things which are more important to your work cause.

The details that are important or redundant to your results can be different in each case of your work. When you work with a report that consists of some data that you have to process, maybe small attention to the data that you have and the analysis method that you have done for completing the report can be crucial to determine whether your report will be good or not. However, if, for example, you put in the attention of the details to the report structure or the narrative typos which are not given too much attention by the people who will be the users of the report, then it can be a waste of time for the work that you do. Even too much checking and rechecking process given to the data or the analysis method can be overkill for the work results that you want. Knowing the balance of giving the micro too much thought and the details that actually must be paid attention can be crucial to ensure that you can do much more in your working day.

If you want to know what kind of details you should pay attention more to, then you should look at the end product that is expected from your work. What is the result that can be considered as great quality for your work? What are the factors that constitute it? It is important that you can see the answers to the questions from the perspective of the people who will directly use the results of your work as your answers for those questions might be different from them. From there, you can think about the micro things which affect the most in your work, the ones that you should pay attention to when you want to go further for the details of your work result. For example, looking at the case of the report that you want to make earlier, maybe you can reflect what are the details that matter in your work from the perspective of your supervisor. Knowing the person, his/her personality, and from your experience dealing with him/her, you might have a clue that your supervisor gives the most attention to the story of the report and the summary that you write as the conclusion of it. So, it is wise to give more attention to the variables that your supervisor thinks are the most important things for the report. An example if you do business might be much more related to what your customers see as the most important factor in your product/service. It will be good if you can conduct some kind of market research first so you know for sure what are the things which are being held as the most important things for your customers that will affect the customer decision to buy or not buy your product/service. The factors which are found prominent to the customer's decision should be the one that you focus your details on compared to the other factors. After all, spending too much time on the things that will not get attention much is surely not a good way to be productive in your work.

But, if you have established some specific variables that you need to pay attention to in your work, then what is the level when it is considered acceptable micro attention and what is the level when it is considered too much attention being given to those variables? Well, you need to think about the appropriate time that should be given to check the details and whether you have exceeded it or not. Before you go check on the details on the variables, it might be wise that you think for a bit on what is the appropriate time that you should give to check on those details? That can be used as a benchmark for you to look to when you do your work. If you have exceeded the time that is given, then it might be the time to stop and move on to other aspects of the works or maybe consider the work done and move on to other works in your to-do list.

The micros can hold some special attention too if you are a supervisor who has some subordinates or employees. The term that is popular here is micromanagement and it holds to when you give in the attention to check and guide the little details in the work of your subordinates/employees. Things like the step-by-step of how to do the work or the very little details of each variable of the work might be something that you still pay attention to when you give the direction and explanation to them. It might not be wise, though, if you keep on micromanaging them like that even though it might be sometimes needed in the special cases when they still do not have enough experience, knowledge, or skills to handle the work that you give on their own and/or the job which is given is found to be quite hard in its level. When it is not special cases like that, it can use much of your time to keep micromanaging everything that is being done by your subordinates/employees. The key here is to establish some level of trust as you keep guiding them until they can work optimally with no to little supervision at all. When you see that they already get some handle of the grip related to their work, then you should be brave enough to let them do some things on their own. Making a habit of micromanaging can only make you lose much more time giving the tasks to them rather than if you work the tasks by yourself. It is because you need to work with them in every detail while they do their work while also checking the work results when they are done. It is certainly overkill and one important thing which you should avoid if you aim to do more in the working hours that you have.

BETTER: NO MORE REDUNDANT TASKS

When we talk about the high productivity that we persevere for, then we should talk also about what kind of work you should do which matters. The time that you spend working on something that is not worth it to be worked on at the first place is a total waste of time. That time that you spend to do that task should be allocated on other more important tasks. When you are able to do that every time, this is what you can call the productivity that you should aim for in your work. This is the Better approach principle from the Do More Better Faster that we should implement to achieve the highest productivity.

Try to reflect on the tasks that you have accomplished in the past and see whether all of them are actually necessary for you to do. Are some of them not relevant to the things that you want to achieve in your work? Do some of them seem to be not important and can actually be neglected without hurting your progress in the work process? When you have some works that seem to be redundant for you, then you should try to not do the same kinds of works again in the future if it seems that you do not need them to get the important work results. Be careful because some of these redundant tasks might already stick themselves to your work habit that it can be hard for you to detect and dismiss them.

This matter is relevant with the earlier example of non-productive work about attending project meetings. You might have the habit of attending all meetings in the projects that you are involved in although some of the meetings do not discuss the part of the project that you actively work on. This can happen because the people in your office usually give an invitation to all of the participants in the project regardless of the project area. You might think that you must attend them all but it might be better if you save the time that you use for attending some of the meetings to do other things in your work. If you want an update on the things discussed in the meetings, then you can ask other people who attended them for a quick recap on things that are being discussed. Being selective on the things that you spend the part of your working hours for is something essential to have high productivity which you can use to produce better work results.

As a person who likes to put in the effort in everything that you do, you might think that working on all the opportunities which are shown up to you is a good thing because that means you have not missed anything that might be important. However, doing something like that will take a lot of time from your working hours as the time will keep on being spent on the things that might have much less priority than the other works on the list. Trying to take a look at the tasks that show themselves to you and see whether those things should be accomplished or you better use your time working on other tasks should be crucial in making your working time optimally used.

After all, we can see this example of focusing on the important things also anywhere when we see the cases of hugely successful people. They simply do not like spending time on redundant activities. Steve Jobs and Mark Zuckerberg, for example, famously wear the same style of clothes almost every day because it is said that they do not want to take too much time on things as trivial as picking the clothes to wear. Warren Buffet also popularly said that the real difference between successful and very successful people is the ability to say yes only to the things that seriously matter while Peter Drucker also said that there is nothing more useless for you than doing efficiently on the things that should not be done at all. The principle has been agreed by many others who have reached their success and it is one thing that you should remember too at work because you must allocate your productivity only on the meaningful works to get meaningful results.

There is also the Pareto principle which is famous in explaining the causal effect relationship. The principle says that often in everything, 20% of the causes are usually responsible for 80% of the results. In the application of the Pareto principle at work, that means that 20% of our work contributes to 80% of the work results that we get. If we just focus our productivity for the completeness of that 20% hugely impactful workload that we have, then it should be much better for us because that means we give our primary attention to the things that give a huge effect on the results that we want from our work.

When you think about it, there might even be some works that show up to us but do not give any effect to the end results that we want. For example, if we have a business and we try to promote our product/service through media where there is little to no customer segmentation that we target. Doing this activity means we have wasted our time trying to work on something that brings zero impact to the result that we want which is improving the sales in our business. By allocating the time that we have to only work on the things that give impact, it should be nice for the progress of producing the results that we want from our labor.

However, how to do this Better approach so we can work only on things that are meaningful for the results that we want? In the next five chapters, we will talk about the application of the suggestions that should improve our productivity in the Better approach. Those suggestions in brief are:

- Do the things that are the most important for you first
- Commit and know how to say "No" on unimportant tasks
- Track the progress that you have for the success you want
- Improve yourself only on the things that matter
- Try to get feedback from your work sooner

Why they are important in doing the Better approach and how we can implement them correctly? I will try to answer those questions for you in the following parts of the book.

BETTER 1: DO THE MITS EARLY

Among the tasks that you have to do on a working day, there have got to be some tasks which seem to be more important than any other tasks. If you want to optimize your time to do the things that matter, then you can do worse than trying to finish those tasks which have the most importance to them early. That way, you can make sure that those tasks are already finished before you do other things that might be not that important to you and those other less important tasks do not prevent you to complete the more important ones.

This is mostly related to the prioritization of the tasks that you have in hand. When using the right to-do list as being suggested in the previous chapter of More approach, try to think also about 2-3 tasks that seem to be more important than the others. It might be the things that are closely related to the end targets of your work or the things that seem need to be finished immediately in your work because of the deadline. Either way, it will be good if you can separate them among all others and do them straight when you start your working hours so you can spend the optimal time needed for figuring out the best results for those tasks.

Being able to complete the most important tasks early can have some other benefits besides being able to finish the most meaningful works before you need to chow down on the others. As you start your working hours, you are often in your most fresh state to begin your work so by doing the most important tasks first, you can make sure that you do your very best in the process to finish them. Your mind should still be in its most focus for work and that can help you in producing your best work on that day. Besides that, the most important tasks that you need to do in your work are most probably something that you keep thinking about if you have not finished them yet. By finishing them earlier before you move on to the other tasks, you make sure that you will clear your mind from the thought of have not finished them as you work through the other tasks.

When you try to separate the most important tasks from the others, think about the impact that each of the tasks has on the results that you want to get. You should ask some questions like: If I do the tasks well, will the results lead me to complete the required things to reach the big targets in my work? If I accomplish these tasks, will it matter greatly to the people who are related to my work targets? After you view the impacts of the task that you have using those kinds of questions, then you should have a clearer idea of whether that thing is something that you should prioritize in your workday. The ones that are not answered favorably to those questions that you ask should be done after you have finished the ones that seem much more important for you.

If you have many tasks and you feel hard to determine which one is the most important than the others despite asking those questions, then you might want to make a list and try to assess the importance of them by using some kind of scoring. Here are the steps that you might want to take regarding the scoring process:
1. Make a table
2. Note down all the tasks that you have in a working day in the rows of the table's first column
3. Think about the variables which can determine the importance of the tasks and write it down in the header of the columns on the right of the first column
4. If you think that the variables do not have the same weight of importance, then add the comparison of the variables' weight using numbers that represent it in the row below where you write the variables names in each column

5. Begin the scoring of each task according to the assessment of them to each of the variables that you have written on the scale of 1-10

6. After you have done the scoring all of the tasks for all of the variables, multiply each scoring in the variable column if you have weights to those variables and sum the results in each row of the task to get the final score that represents the importance of each task

7. Get the rank for each of the tasks compared to the others. That should be the right base of your prioritization for the most important tasks that you should do earlier that day

As an example of the scoring result, here is an instance of the works done by a person who works on her retail shop in the day

Tasks	Variables			Final Score	Priority
	Impress Customer	Improve Sales	Self-imposed Deadline		
	2	3	5		
Create SOP to greet customer	5	2	3	31	5
Rearrange product interface	3	4	3	33	4
Create next month	2	4	2	26	7

promotion material					
Brief new employees	4	2	5	39	1
Have a meeting with business partner	3	3	4	35	2
Check finance	1	2	3	23	8
Check pricing	1	4	4	34	3
Formulate in-store promotion	1	4	3	29	6

Looking at the table and the final score which has been given to all the tasks, then the most important tasks for her should be to brief new employees, meet her business partner to discuss the evaluation and improvement of the store, and check the pricing that is being implemented. Those tasks, then, should be the ones that she works on as soon as she gets the chance in the day, starting from the one with the highest score.

When you make the tables to determine your most important tasks, you might want to keep notes on the variables that are used for your scoring of the tasks too. You might need them in the next time you use the table to identify your most important tasks later in other days. This is because most probably, the variables that you want to write will be more or less the same with what you have used before.

BETTER 2: SAY FIRM "NO" TO UNNECESSARY JOBS

As has been told earlier when we discuss the Better part from the Do More Better Faster approach, it is important for you to not do anything which is redundant in your work and focus yourself on doing only the things that are meaningful to the targets that you want to reach. Therefore, it is very important that you can recognize what are the redundant jobs that come up in your way and what you can do to be able to say no strongly to those which seem to only take up your time without contributing anything to the results that you want.

It is sometimes hard to say no especially to something which seems very interesting to do or when the works come from someone that you have known well. When it comes to helping a person, you can help if you think that the person really needs your help, it is in the area which you can contribute much for, and it does not sacrifice what you want to do in terms of your own work too much. However, you should prioritize the works that can bring you to progress to the targets that you want as doing things that are not related to them can be considered as wasting your time and lower much of your productivity. Even when it comes to something that seems interesting, you must be eager to say no to it if it does not help you to reach the end targets that you want to realize.

If you want to identify whether the work that comes up to you is redundant or not, then you can ask some of these questions to help you:

- Is the work in line with the targets that you have in terms of your work?

- Is the work worth it to be completed considering the time that you need to sacrifice to do it?
- If you look back later and evaluate what you have done in your working hours today, will finishing this work be something that you consider as productive?
- Is the work within your area of responsibility?
- If the work is not done, then will it affect badly for you in the present or in the future?

When you answer all of the questions with a positive note, then it should be something that is necessary for you to do. The ones with mostly negative answers to those questions should be considered as redundant and you should think seriously whether you need to spend your time doing it at all.

When you can say no to the unimportant things at work, then there should be many benefits that you can have. Besides the benefit of having your working hours spent well as you allocate them for something which can give you meaningful results, you should be able to work with less stress and fewer things to think about when you dismiss all the unimportant things in your work. More works that you have to do means more things to figure out and by reducing the unimportant workloads, it should reduce your stress too. You can also build the habits of working on the essential things only and that will be great for you in the long run when there can be more responsibilities that come in your way. You should improve yourself in selecting the works that can bring you closer to the targets that you want to realize. Doing only the things that matter should also make you much faster to achieve the success that you want at work.

Now, that we have already understood more about the importance of selecting only the right works and how to select them, it is the matter of learning how to say no. Say no can be hard because you may feel uneasy either to yourself or to other people if you are being asked to do the work by them. Saying no to yourself is more related to overcome the feeling of missed opportunities and guilt that can accompany when you choose to not doing some tasks. What can you do to say firm no for yourself? There are some suggestions which you can implement:

- **Remind yourself about the end targets that you want to achieve at work**. When you seriously want to succeed in work, then you should try to eliminate the tasks that are not related to it as much as possible. Think about the success that you want to achieve and note to yourself that dismissing the work is actually necessary to progress faster to success

- **Remember again that time is precious and a limited resource**. The time that you have spent on something can never be got back and used to do another thing. Therefore, you can assure yourself that you have done the right thing if you use your working hours only to work on the matters that are important and meaningful to you

- **Think of the no that you give as the personal growth that you need**. The things that you do for work productivity are needed to make you a better person especially in terms of time management. The rejection that you give to redundant tasks should be good to make you get used to work on productive activities only

Another target of saying no is the person that you have to tell it to. You have to be firm in it so it leaves no doubt for the person about the rejection that you have made while also take care of the person's feelings too so you do not break the relationship. If there is ever the moment when it feels not good to reject some works from a person, then here are some things that you can do:

- **Say sorry and present some appreciation**. Sorry gives the indication that you regret you are unable to take the chance and appreciation will present the other person's offer as something good for you although you cannot take it at the moment. Try to begin the no with sorry and say appreciation on how great the offer is and how considerate the person thinks of you as someone who is given the chance to do the work.

- **Give an acceptable reason**. When you reject something, the reason is always important as it explains to the person why you are unable to take the chance. The real reason might be that you consider what the person offers as something redundant for you to do but it is obviously too frontal if you give a reason like that. Think and give a reason that you feel acceptable and logical to the person depending on the rejection condition.

- **Provide some kind of compensation**. Compensation is always nice when given appropriately. Look at the situation and provide compensation that fits it. Something which might be small but relevant from your thinking can also be nice when it is being said to the person to redeem the rejection (e.g. promise to consider other work invitations in the future, offer to allocate some time outside working hours to give your insight which can be useful about the work)

Say no can sometimes be hard for us and to other people that we reject although it is necessary so you can allocate your working hours to much more important tasks. However, do not be deterred to do it when the work is redundant because it is also important to allocate the time resource that you have for something from which the results matters.

BETTER 3: KEEP TRACK OF THE SUCCESS MEASUREMENT

Well, this is related heavily to the success that you want to achieve through your work. When you have already defined the success that is meaningful to you and you are serious in accomplishing the achievement, then you should also define the measurement that you can keep track of daily or in other periods when you want to evaluate your progress to the success. By doing that, you should be able to keep an eye on the works that you do, whether it is relevant to the progress that you want to make to succeed while also applying the Better approach that is important for high work productivity. You can also measure the contribution that your work results give to bring you closer to your targets.

Hence, this is part of why it is very important too to make your targets tangible and measurable as being suggested in the earlier chapter. When you define the cause of your work, make sure it has a quantitative output attached to it so you can easily see the impact of your work on the cause.

One thing that you also need to remember when you want to keep track of the success measurement is that it should be compared also to the gradual targets and milestones that you may have set related to the success that you want to achieve. The gradual targets and milestones should be nearer to you than your end success and they should be able to be achieved in less time. By trying to look into them, you can make sure that you are on target to achieve them which means you are on target to achieve the end success that you want too. Gradual targets and milestones can be much more measurable to you when keeping track of the success measurement compared to if you only directly compare your work results to the end success that you want.

So, when you allocate your hours to work on something, think about how the results may affect the progress measurement to your success. Will the result of your work be something that becomes quantifiable in the end and help to support you in terms of the numbers that you associate with the achievements that you want? If it is not, then you might consider the work as something that you should not do because it cannot help you to progress. Do only the things that can support you to add up to those important numbers as much as possible. It can be a direct or indirect additional number but the most important thing is that they contribute to the things that you want to achieve. Any work which does not have that kind of nature should be thought over again because it may be a waste of your time and the opposite of productivity when you do it.

From the assessment of the number addition that might add up for the achievement of your end success, you can also think about the prioritization that you have to do regarding your tasks. The things that have more importance are the ones that can be expected to contribute the largest to your numbers. When you want to measure the impact size of your work, this is one of the things that you must do. It will be very good if you have some strong bases of why you expect the numbers that you predict to come up from the results of your work. For example, you may reasonably expect the promotion that you do in an event for your product to improve your sales at a certain number because you have some historical data that says that you can expect the average conversion rate from the predicted number of visitors for the event to your sales. This kind of thing should make you surer that you can achieve the numbers that are expected from the activities that you choose to do in your working hours.

However, you may think that you already have your hands full with your work during the working hours that it is hard to reflect on the works that you have done and the works that you are going to do to keep track of them for your success measurement. What can you do about it? Well, you can allocate a little time before you end your day or at the beginning of the working day when you have not started your working hours. If you have got some time that you can allocate for doing the to-do list as has been recommended in the previous chapter, then it will be nicer if you can do the success measurement for your work around that time too. Reflect on the work that you have done in the previous day and what you can do so you can optimize your work in the next day with the things that can help you in improving your progress in your quantified success significantly.

You may also want to measure your progress in some regular period other than daily, probably quarterly, so you can reflect in a larger picture to the things that you have done in the previous period and what you can do to improve your numbers in the next period before the evaluation is done again. You may want to allocate a bigger time for this in a day, probably half an hour to an hour in a day when you do not work such as weekends, so you can think more clearly and can gain the optimum benefit from your reflection activity. Do not forget to reflect against your progress to the gradual targets or milestones that you have got too when you are at it.

The measurement that you do to the expected work results can be the activity that opens your eyes to the things that you should do so you can apply the Better approach more intensely. Be truthful and strict about it. If the work does not seem to be able to add up the numbers for your progress to succeed then even though it seems interesting, then you must

have the commitment to allocate your time for other things
that can be more useful for you.

BETTER 4: SHARPEN THE RIGHT KNIFE

What are the areas or the works which you think are the most important for you to achieve success? Maybe they are something which you have done that have given significant results for you in the past or the things that you do in the present or will do in the future that seems to be crucial for the achievements that you want to accomplish at work. Whatever they are, you should think about how can you improve yourself so you can do those seemingly significant parts of your work in a much better way. Hence, you can get more optimum results in the works that matter the most to you as a result. That is the kind of lesson that you should learn if you want to improve yourself productively.

The objectives of professional learning activities are to gain knowledge and skills that will be useful to be implemented at work. However, it can be that what you learn does not give any impact at all and does not bring the progress needed to the realization of your success that you want because those lessons do not make much impact on the works that matter. After you have identified what are the tasks that are the most meaningful in improving your chance to success from the previous chapters in the Better approach, you should try to improve your way to do those things so you can amplify the results that are produced from them. Remember the 80/20 principle of Pareto? It is better that you keep sharpening the knife for the areas that prove significant for you and give 80% of the results that you want rather than doing it for the ones that only give 20% of the results.

What can you do to sharpen your knife in your most important works? Well, there are many options that are available to improve your knowledge and skills significantly.

As technology has gone to become more established in our life, the option of online learning can be done if you want to be able to do it anytime anywhere. The sources that you can use for developing your capability in your works are vast, with the choices come from the media of webinars, online courses, articles, video tutorials, groups or forums, e-books, to some other options which you can utilize.

There are also excellent offline education media that you can use for the purpose. Things like seminars, training, courses, reading books are among the things that you can use to develop yourself. It is a matter of determining what are the factors that seem like the most important to you when it comes to learning. If you prefer the flexibility of place and time, then you might prefer to learn online. However, if you prefer to meet with other people who have the same background or consult directly with the lesson's instructors, then the offline education will be better suit for you.

When trying to learn more to improve yourself, you can also meet and discuss with other people who may have more knowledge, skills, and experience on the things that you want to develop yourself in. Direct discussions with the people that you know might be more beneficial in terms of the specific competencies that you want to learn. You can ask directly about the things that you want to know or probably even being instructed directly on how to do things in your work if the lessons require you to practice. Just make sure that you have asked a considerable and fair amount of time from them to learn about the things that are important for you so they do not mind giving the optimal lessons for you and you can prepare beforehand on the things that you want to learn within that timeframe.

When you try to sharpen the right knife in your work, what are other things that you must consider to do your learning in a productive way? Here are some pointers which can be useful:

- **Allocate some time and (probably) money to maximize the learnings that you get**. Learning the right things requires concentration to understand them and doing it also might require you to spend some money to get the best lessons. Allocate regular time for you to do the learning activities and budget a little part from your income to support your learning activities. Be sure to spend them on the excellent education in the areas which contribute the most in your work so the time and money are not used in vain

- **Learn your skills from credible sources.** Professional skills require some expertise and know-how capability to make the people give the lessons that can have high possibilities to be effective when you implement them. Find credible sources from where the professional knowledge and skills are given before deciding to take the lessons that are being offered to you.

- **Understand your optimal way of learning**. Some people might be visual learners, meaning that they learn more effectively when they learn by seeing the instructions of the lessons, auditory, the ones who learn more effectively through the lessons primarily given by what they can hear, or have other kinds of learning method which suit them the most. Know yours by reflecting on the times that you have understood in the most effective way in the past and try to sharpen the right knife of yours in the media to significantly improve your understanding process.

- **Take note (by writing) of the lessons that you get**. Research shows that taking notes by hand on pieces of paper can improve your memory retention on the lessons that are given to you. Therefore, keep your notebook and pen close by when you do your learning activities. When you find things that are interesting and seem important, take them out and start writing on those points for your improved way of learning. Besides, the things that you note can also be seen at a later time when you want to implement the lessons and need some references to them.

- **Know the aspects that you want to learn**. Before you begin your learning activities, think about the details of things that you want to know from them. Doing that can focus your time on focusing for the things that matter on the area and if you have an instructor in the learning activities, then you can ask about those aspects also if it has not been covered during the lessons teaching time

However, the most important thing after getting the knowledge and skills from your learning activities is, of course, making sure that you implement them in your work. By doing that as soon as possible, you will know the impact of the knowledge and skills that you have learned and can apply them consistently in your work if they prove to be useful in improving your productivity and work results quality.

BETTER 5: COLLECT THE FEEDBACK SOONER

The work results that you produce are used by other people, whether it is your boss, peers, subordinate, customer, or maybe other people who have interest in the things that you do. It is very possible that the thing that you work on will not be perfect for the first time asking. Therefore, the sooner you can collect the feedback on your work result, the better and faster it should be for it to take shape into the results that can satisfy or even exceed the expectation of the people who use them.

Ever heard of the term MVP in the area of product development? The long version of it is the "Minimum Viable Product" and that is what you should pursue in your work if the condition allows it to be. There might be times when you can only submit your work once and you cannot correct it afterward such as when there is a tight deadline for your work and the current time is already near the deadline. When the condition is like that, then you may not be able to get some feedback for your work before you deliver the final version of it. However, most of the time there should be some space when you can finish the work and have it shown first to the people who can give a relevant assessment for the formulation of the final work results. Try to not miss the opportunity to do that as the improvement that you do based on the feedback can be the crucial one which determines whether the work is going to be a success or not.

However, do the work as fast as you can so you can collect the feedback does not mean that you can give a bad work for the first version of the result. On the opposite, you should try to produce the best thing that you can do so, if possible, the improvement that you need to do should be not too major as such that you have to redo most of the work. If you have got or made some kind of deadline for the final version of your work, then you should try to give yourself some mini-deadlines for the work results that you try to get the feedback from. During the time until that mini-deadlines, work as best as you can to produce the best results to ask people's feedbacks from.

There are many benefits that you can have by trying to get the feedbacks to the MVP form of your work results as fast as you can. First of all, obviously, the final work result that you submit will have been tested in terms of its quality. When you give the final version to the stakeholders who will get a direct impact from it, it should be close to the best that can be expected. You can also save time in terms of guessing what are the things that you need to do to satisfy the expectation of the users. Rather than figuring out by thinking of it by yourself which probably will be wrong, you can get the thinking from relevant people who know better about the aspects which should be paid attention to in your work result. Besides these, you may also gain more perspectives about what are the things that you need to do in those specific aspects of your work to produce the best results for you.

This is in line with the Better approach in our high productivity effort as we will try to work *only* on the aspects that matter in our work. You may not know what they are until you get feedbacks from the people whose opinion matter. By getting the grasp of those aspects as soon as possible, you may save your working hours significantly by not spending them too much on the unimportant factors which do not influence what defines as the excellence for your product/service.

In trying to get the evaluation process from other people to your work results, you must also think about who are the people who you want to get the feedback from so you get the opinion that matters for the improvement of your work results. You do not want to get opinions from just whoever people that you can find because doing so might lead the improvement that you do to the work results wrongly. Therefore, if you cannot get the feedback directly from the direct users of your product/service (probably because the user is your boss who is very hard to reach for the feedback or the users are actually customers who are so many in terms of the number of people), then you should try to get the feedback from the people who can represent the opinion from those direct users. If there are not too many people who you expect to be the direct users of your work results, then you might want to ask the feedback from the people who seem to understand well about the opinion that the direct users will give or the people who seem to have the same preferences of aspects in a work result. However, if there are many people who will use your work results (customers), then you can ask feedback from a group of people who seem to have the same characteristics or background with those end-users. Ultimately, it will be best if you can get feedback from the direct users of your work results as they are the ones who know best whether your work is already good or not, and if not, what are the aspects that you should improve so it can be good.

Understanding what you need to do in your work to produce the results that can be considered as the best should be the thing that you do as soon as possible. Doing your best and fastest for the work results that can be called your MVP and asking feedbacks for them can be the right way to do that and make you work on only the things that matter to the results.

FASTER: NO MORE SLOW EXECUTION

The last approach from the Do More Better Faster is the Faster approach. This is the art of getting things done as quickly as possible without compromising the quality.

After all, this is one of the main essences of having high productivity, right? That is being able to do your tasks as quickly as possible. After learning about how you utilize your working hours mostly for working, do more jobs at the same time, and work on only the things that matter, you need to also understand how to do your work faster. Having the habit to do that while maintaining the goodness of the results should make you be able to allocate the time that you save from your work for other things that are important for you. Moreover, you should also be able to achieve the end targets in your work faster because you can finish the workloads that become the requirement of them quicker too. As a result, logically, you can accomplish the success that you aim in your work earlier than you expect it to be. Thus, the high speed of your work can bring some benefits to the things that you want which are clear to see.

After all, time is a precious resource and you only have a limited amount of it in a day. Every second count and it is favorable that you can do what you have to do by spending as least amount of time as possible. When you are able to finish things faster, that should bring you many advantages in trying to utilize this time resource as well. You are able to complete work in a shorter period compared to the others and that should give you more time to allocate to be able to produce more excellent results for other tasks that you have to do.

However, you should not forget that you should also keep an eye on the quality of your work outcome when trying to speed up the process. A below standard result that is caused by the faster process that you bring to your job cannot be good also because that means that you will have to spend much time also doing the improvement of it or even need to redo it because that work result is not acceptable at all. Always pay attention to the quality aspect of your work and try to not take the shortcut that can speed up the process but also lower the quality of the work results significantly.

To do the speed improvement process right, there are some variables that you must consider when you try to speed up your work. When you talk about how to do things fast, then you might also want to mention the concentration that your mind has regarding the things that you work on. This is because the two things seem to correlate to one another. A greater concentration that you have when you do something should bring to you a greater speed to finish it without lacking quality in the outcome.

There might be a question that comes to your mind: Why more concentration in your work can bring more speed factor to it? Here is an illustration: Have you ever got experience when you had a very difficult task to do at work that also has a tight deadline attached to it? This is a very stressful thing to have indeed. If you have this kind of experience, then remember what do you typically do when you are in that kind of situation? I figure one of the things that you do is block the other works that you have to concentrate on finishing this one hard task that must be completed as soon as possible. Now, why do you do that? That is because, instinctively, you might realize that by concentrating on fewer things, you should be able to get the jobs done quicker. Compare the situation to if you need to use your mind thinking on many tasks that you have to do and you should be able to see much difference.

A greater focus on your work can bring many advantages in terms of finishing it quickly and that is one of the important things that you should note when you try to do your tasks with high productivity. Therefore, you should try to think of your work one at a time to be able to optimize the speed of your work significantly. After all, if you can do the work faster, then you should be able to move on to other tasks quickly too.

Besides concentration, the more experience that you have in the work process should also make you able to do it faster. As you add more know-how in your repertoire when you do more things related to the tasks that you have, naturally, you should be able to do it more effectively and efficiently. That is because you become more knowledgeable in going straight to the aspects which are essential to be done in your work. This will cause you to finish the work faster and doing so with a better result.

The knowledge of the aspects of the work that you should do is important so you can spend less time and give more quality in general. That required knowledge can be applied also with knowing the things that you should do in the period that you have in your working hours. Not knowing the important activities might bring you to fill time with figuring out what are the things that you should do in the time that you have and that can make you slower in terms of moving from task to task.

So, after knowing the variables that you need to speed up the process in your work significantly, what can you do to amplify those variables to support you? These are the suggestions that you can implement regarding this Faster approach to improve your productivity significantly:

- Immerse to the unique flow of your work
- Formulate a work schedule that you implement with discipline
- Set aside repetitive tasks and see the chance to automate them
- Focus on one task and one task only in a time
- Do the important and relevant work multiple times

We will discuss these five things deeper in the next chapters for you to understand them more, starting with the first one.

FASTER 1: GET INTO THE FLOW

Have you got into a situation during your work in which you feel your mind is fully focused on the task that you have at hand and you seem to go along optimally with the time to be able to complete that work of yours? You must have experienced something quite like that at some points in the past, although you may not realize it. And no, this is not some kind of freaky superpower if you have not remembered something quite like that yet during your past working experience. It is actually something which is often called the flow state of your work and you can get into this kind of state if you have a high concentration with the task that you have at hand.

To simplify its definition, this flow is the state of work condition when you can work in your most optimum capability. It is the ideal work situation that brings the best out of you and thus, you should try to do your job in that kind of situation as much as possible because doing that can make you much faster in completing the work while maintaining or even improving the resulting quality. It is the moment when you feel like every effort that you put in your work just comes out naturally and thus, this state can surely bring a high speed out of you to produce your work results.

This state might be more apparent to people when they do something like writing a book. When it comes to writing a book, then the flow is the situation when the words seem to just come out from your mind and you just there to type them non-stop. When you are in your optimum condition, it may feel that the work which you do at the moment seems like something that is just naturally done. This can be because you just go with the flow in your mind to finish it as soon as possible. In the state flow, you just lose yourself and become immersed with your work that you might not know how much time has passed as you enjoy putting in the effort on your work.

Well, it seems like the flow state can bring a great benefit in terms of enforcing the Faster approach in your quest to achieve high productivity on something that you do. So, what can you try to get into the flow of your work and enter the realm of this optimum speed? The most important thing is that you need to have your concentration solely on the work that you do. The practical pieces of advice in the Do approach when you want to stay away from all of the significant distractions at work can also be used to help you in this too. Bring yourself to the highest focus that your mind can have and you should be able to enter the flow after some time you are at work. Some people said that it takes at least 10-15 minutes for you to be able to enter the flow state since the start of your work. During that period, you must keep undivided attention to the thing that you do and focus only on one task, not more.

When you try to start your work and enter the state of the flow, it may feel hard for you to do it and the early minutes may seem so boring for you that you might be easily distracted with other things that come in your way. However, do not stop at that point and keep on going so you can work in the flow state. The commitment to work in a considerable period is needed if you want to utilize that kind of moment in your work.

If you are not discipline and do not have strong discipline, though, it can be easy for you to break the commitment anytime during the period as you get disrupted by other things outside your work. So, what you can do to be able to work within the flow in a considerable time? Here are some things that you can do for it:

- **Work in the place where you can be sure to have as minimum distractions as possible**. Getting to the state of flow requires you to do your work uninterrupted for a period of time. Moving your work to the place with the lowest possible of disruption during your task's accomplishment can be the best thing for you to keep on doing your job.

- **Let other relevant people around you know that you try to work without disruption for some period of time.** A person who does not know that you want to do your job continuously in some duration might distract you by coming to you for a chit chat or something else. Letting the people that you think might distract you during your flow know about your intention to concentrate can be good in your quest to maintain your focus.

- **Keep the irrelevant things to the work that you want to do away for a while**. Doing work uninterrupted might be harder if there are things around you that can distract you from your work, such as your gadget or probably the novel that you have not finished reading yet. Try to move the things which are not fit with the purpose of your work to support your effort to work consistently.

- **Arrange your work and break time**. You may feel a burnout thus cannot focus on the flow if you keep on doing your work for a very long time. Therefore, if you need it, it is important too to alternate the time that you have between work and break. Popular switching techniques between them, like the Podomoro technique (work 25 minutes and break for 5 minutes) or the 52/17 rule (work 52 minutes and break for 17 minutes) can be tried and implemented for your work rhythm to make it easier to manage your focus on work

However, it might be hard to do it if your current work requires you to discuss with your peers or make you need to be in a place where there are many distractions. Therefore, you must try to look at the situation and apply the suggestions whenever possible so you can see the effect and able to enter the state of flow as much as possible when you want to get a highly productive time from the working hours that you have.

FASTER 2: MAKE A PRECISE SCHEDULE

When it comes to knowing what you want to do in a day, as being stated in the previous chapter as something that can support the Faster approach, it may be good to reflect back on the daily to-do list that you might have implemented in your work from the More approach. If you want to use the tool, then to drive you to improve the speed of your work, it can be useful to formulate a specific schedule for the things which you have listed in your to-do list.

Why does a specific schedule can help you to do things faster? The first reason is, of course, the precise knowledge of what you should do and the ideal time that should be allocated for you to do the work. By having an understanding of that, you can have more motivation to finish the work by not exceeding the time that you have for it because doing that might push the other works that you already pack in your schedule. The late work can make the work results which you plan to accomplish become messy. You might even want to finish the work much faster than the period that you have allocated in your schedule for the work so you can start working on other things earlier.

The second reason is the consistency that it can give to your work if you implement your schedule constantly and disciplined. By having work consistency, there will be some improvement in the speed of thought as you get used more to the work rhythm that moves you from one work to another. Because of that, you might be able to improve the speed of your work further as time goes by so you can be even more productive in the jobs that you do.

The third reason is related to the commitment that you have to something that you have made yourself. You might be lazy to do things that are given by others but you should be more committed to doing the things that you decide for yourself. By formulating the work schedule that allocates your working hours on the works that you yourself think should be done in that day, you should have more push to accomplish the promise that you have made to yourself and thus, that will make you speed up your work to meet the time commitment that you have made in your schedule.

The guidance that a daily schedule can give seems to be important in your work. Therefore, you might want to try to spare some time to formulate it before you go to your working days. Probably during the time when you formulate your to-do list which means at the end of the previous day or at the start of the working day. Think about what are the things that you should do and what is the duration that you need to finish each of them. As has been described for the MITs of your work, allocate the working hours that you have first and foremost to the most important tasks that you have to do.

Regarding the specific duration that you need to give to the work activities, you may want to be pretty detailed so the schedule can become the guide which is not abstract when you want to look at it during the day. You can try the time frame of fifteen minutes which means that you should be precise in the period that you allocate for your work to the time frame of fifteen minutes. Give the time for each of your work which is aggressive and also realistic so it will motivate you to finish the work fast but the duration should be possible looking at the size of the workload. That way, the schedule should be able to give an able support to your Faster approach.

If you want to be better in terms of making the precise work schedule, then it will be good if you can spend time to build a weekly and daily schedule on the things that you have to do beforehand. Do the weekly schedule first as you are on the verge of entering the relevant work week and look again at the schedule while refining them as needed when you approach the day. A week should be enough for you to know the general time that you have for work in that period. Formulating the weekly schedule first might help you to keep the works more on track to the targets and milestones that you have in your work and enable you to see the big picture of your work too. Refining it daily should be good as you may not know the exact detail of the working hours that you have on that day until the day before or at the beginning of the day. By implementing this kind of method when you formulate your schedule, you should be able to optimize more of the working hours that you have in the span of the working days' weeks. Keep the daily schedules that you have made in a note that you can see. The note should also be put close to you during work so you can see it whenever you need some guidance regarding what are the things that you need to do in the working hours that you have.

However, there might be some cases in your working hours that a very urgent task suddenly comes up which seems to need you to spend some period to accomplish it. When you happen to experience this, try to see whether this task which seems very urgent has to actually be done by you. It might be the case that the task seems urgent but not important for you to do or it is something that should be done by someone else, e.g. your subordinates or your peers. If you have taken a look at it and decide that it is something that you should do immediately, then you can see the schedule that you have and determines what can be changed for it to accommodate the sudden and urgent work. Note that this should only be done when it is an absolute must and you have no other choices. If it is not, then you should stick to your work schedule and do not use the task that suddenly comes up as something to make you get away from the things that you should do according to the schedule.

Try to be consistent in formulating and implementing the schedule and you should get better in time to optimize your working hours using the tool. It might be hard to be discipline at first but the impact can be great for the Faster approach of your productivity if you are committed enough to make this into a habit.

FASTER 3: CUT OUT REPETITIVE TASKS (AUTOMATE IF POSSIBLE)

Your tasks which are monotonous and repetitive can take a considerable part of your working hours if you do not pay attention. They can make you occupied and refrain you from doing other things which might be more important for you. This can be the case if you let yourself fall into the routine of your repetitive tasks every day in your working hours. Hence, it will be good if you can spend some time to identify what are the things that can be considered as repetitive tasks in your work and cut them out from your work, either by allocating the completion of them in the same time so you can work on them simultaneously or leave them out completely if you see that they have no to little importance to the work results that you want to chase. If they prove to have some importance and when it is an appropriate case, then you might also want to do automation to those tasks so they can be completed even if you do not give special attention to them.

Repetitive tasks are the works that we repeat many times throughout our working days and can be also be defined as the things that you do without having to think much. Repetitive tasks can be found in each of our work. They can be something which seem small but we work on them by spending a lot of time if we add up the period that we utilize for them in our working days. If you work in an office, then checking your email or doing data entry might be the things that you do that can be considered repetitive. If you work on your own business, then scanning the performance of your business or doing some approvals on the things that your employees do can also be seen as monotonous works. In doing them separately and with a considerable amount of time for each task, you can lose the opportunity to work on much more productive jobs which may have more impact for you than these tasks.

Repetitive tasks are considered to be a burden to productivity these days and should be the things that are completed without allocating too much time to them. According to the research done by SnapLogic, 90 percent of employees are being burdened by these kinds of tasks which they consider to be boring and repetitive. The research which is accomplished by McKinsey also tells us similar things. It says that in about 60 percent of occupations, at least one-third of the activities can be considered as repetitive and should be automated. The research also tells us that over 40 percent of the workers who are surveyed spend at least a quarter of their workweek to do repetitive tasks. If we can trim out or even automate the tasks which can be considered as repetitive, then it should be a significant boost to our productivity especially in the Faster approach that we discuss.

So, you should reflect on your work in the past and evaluate what are the things that you do which can be considered as repetitive looking at the definition for it above. After you have tried to recollect them, see what are the things that you can do to make them finished much more effectively and efficiently. After all, these are the things that should be able to be done without thinking too much when working on them, right? As the things that you should do to those repetitive tasks, you can:

- Assign them to someone else whose responsibilities are lower and include these repetitive tasks or someone outside of the organization structure (do outsourcing) who has the capability to do them if you have the authority to do delegate the tasks
- Remove them altogether from the things that you have to do if you see that the results of these works

have no to very little contribution to the overall results that you want from your work process

- Group them together to work on in one part of your working hours so you can utilize the flow state of your work to be able to complete them faster
- Automate the works if appropriate

When it comes to doing automation to the repetitive tasks, then technology comes in a big part for the help as you try to streamline the process in the works. There are things like a system built especially to do the tasks or machine learning technology which can automate your works, particularly those which are related to data. To pick the best automation solution, you have to take a look at some factors which are related to the tasks. The things that you have to consider are suggested in the step-by-step as follows:

1. **What kind of automation that can be done to the repetitive tasks?**

   Take a look deeper into the repetitive tasks that you want to automate and see the aspects in them which can benefit immensely from the automation. Different tasks may require different solutions to them.

2. **What are the alternatives for the automation process?**

   After you have recognized the kind of automation process that best suits your needs by fitting it with the important aspects of the repetitive tasks, you have to take a look at the options available to do the automation process. Examine and make a note to the kinds of technology and vendors which can answer to your problems

3. **What are the benefits that you can get from each of the alternatives?**

   See the advantages that you can have from all of those technologies and vendors. You might want to make a note of them also so you can compare them clearly for the base of your choice

4. **What are the costs that you have to spend for each of the alternatives?**

   Understand the price that you have to pay regarding the procurement of the alternatives. Besides the obvious thing such as the initial financial cost, you may also want to see about the financial cost that can incur to maintain the automation process and other costs such as the time that you need to install and adapt to the automation system or the people that you need to have to watch over the process. Compare it with the benefit that you assess earlier

5. **Which one is the best choice for your tasks?**

   After you compare the benefit and cost of each alternative, choose the one which seems to give you the best value. Be disciplined in the implementation for the automation system so you can get the best benefits from it in the long run

If you are an employee, then to have the automation process system, you might need to sound a proposal to the people in the office who are responsible for the automation procurement decision. If you have a compelling case and they see that the automation will bring much improvement in terms of productivity and the quality of the work results, then you should be confident that the automation can happen. It might even be the things that your company actually needs to get much better results in its product/service while also optimizing its employees' output significantly.

FASTER 4: AVOID MULTITASKING

Multitasking is a myth. That is one important thing that you should engrave in your mind when you try to improve the speed of your work. Trying to focus on more than one work at a time does not only make your mind cannot have a full concentration. It also makes you unable to optimize the time that you have during your working hours because you cannot work in the highest productivity that you can be on the jobs that you have to do by doing multitasking.

The fact is that you can only focus on one thing at a time during your work. Research done by Ohio University shows that multitask simply cannot be done. It actually hurts your work performance when you try to do it and it just make you feel emotionally better because you think you are being productive and can finish more things in your work at the same time when the reality is not like that. Earl Miller, a neuroscience professor at MIT, says we simply cannot focus on more than one task at once. What we do when we say that we multitask is actually switching our attention from one task to another back and forth. If we do this task-switching process, we can have a serious disadvantage from the switching cost that we have to pay for our work productivity. Another research which is conducted by Joshua Rubinstein, Jeffrey Evans, and David Meyer from the University of Michigan concludes that we can lose as much as 40 percent of our productivity by the mental block created from doing this task switching. A quite high percentage number which suggests that we should not try to multitask because by doing that, we actually penalize the time that we have in our working hours instead of optimizing it.

Even doing the things which seem simple and straightforward to us can bring a bad effect if we try to multitask them, such as driving and texting. The US

National Transportation Safety Board says that driving while texting at the same time is the same as driving with a blood-alcohol level three times the legal limit. This further reinforces the fact that it is very vital for us to focus on one thing at a time as doing the opposite will bring worse performance from us in either of them.

Restrict the task that you do at a time to just one and allocate the other things that you have to do into the other parts of your working hours. As you have already learned from the description of the flow chapter from the Faster approach, trying to concentrate on one work can also support yourself significantly to bring the optimum state in your mind to do it. This can amplify the speed of the work when you isolate your work process from the others.

So, knowing the bad impact of trying to do multitask and the positive effect for our work speed and result when we focus to work on one thing at a time, we have to commit ourselves to be able to do just that most of the time. If previously we try to do multitask as much as possible because we believe that it can be one of the keys for high productivity, then it is time to try to divide our tasks so they can be done in separate period for each. Changing the mindset that you have significantly regarding multitasking should be crucial to make sure that you strive to not do it again for your future work.

Besides that, in relation to the daily work schedule tool utilization which has been suggested earlier, try to allocate one work at a time for the period that you have in your schedule. Be precise in dividing the things that you should do into one task at a time so you do not confuse and mix the tasks that you have to do in one period, especially when you have already known that doing that can be quite harmful to your productivity. By having the restriction of doing one job at a time, you may also try to allocate less time to the things in your schedule as you only need to do one thing at a time now. Be disciplined about this in your schedule as this tool should be the guidance on what you have to do in your working day.

When it comes to avoiding multitasking, then you need to also consider creating the boundaries that you have between one work and the others. When you try to focus on doing one work only, then keep the things that are relevant to the other works but irrelevant to your current work away from you.

For example, if you are currently working on the part of a project which you have responsibility for, then it will be beneficial for you to close the link to the data analysis file that you have related to the report that you have to formulate for another work or close the links in your browser which might be usable for the source of your presentation material that you have to show in the next two days. Try to be there fully in the work that you currently do and forget other things as much as you can because you should have other time to think about the other works. By restricting your access to the things related to other works, you should be able to focus more on the one work that you do as you reduce the temptation to do other things that are not relevant to your current work.

You might also want to pay attention to the switching cost that has been mentioned earlier as one of the things that can bring a bad impact on your productivity. It may be hard for you to reduce the work switching cost down to zero as you most probably have to work on more than one tasks in your working hours. To keep it to the minimum, however, try to do the task that you have in one period until it is done and do not separate it to different time frames in your working day if it is possible. Grouping the tasks that you have according to its similarity as has been described in the More approach can also help you to reduce the switching cost as there are still some aspects that are at least the same when you change your focus on the other tasks in the grouping.

FASTER 5: DO ITERATION IN ONE AREA

This last suggestion for optimizing your Faster approach is related to the habit of the way you do things at work. As you add more experience on how to accomplish your job, you should have more know-how knowledge on what are the most effective and efficient way to do your work. As a result, the more time passes, the faster you do your work because of the gradual improvement of that knowledge. Things that you have done for a long time might even be quite automatic to you because the knowledge of how to do the job is already embedded itself firmly to your subconscious mind.

Here is an illustration to help you understand that: If you have the ability to drive a car, do you remember when you just start learning how to do it? When you begin to learn how to drive, it might be confusing for you to operate your vehicle so it can move to the direction that you want. You may forget to shift the gear when you need to do it, confused on how to place your foot at the right time on the brake pedal to stop the car, or do not know how to turn on the car wiper or light. As a result, during the early journey of your driving, you may hit something by accident or unable to park your car in the empty parking spot. However, as you add to your experience and begin to know what are the things that you must do so it can be much smoother when you drive, you become more and more adept in your driving skill. Eventually, you even can do it without much thinking. It feels like the process is automatic for you to operate the car and bring it to the destination that you want. You also become much faster to control the things that you need to drive and as a result, you can get to any place in much shorter time too.

That is a simple example of what consistent iterations over a period of time in something can bring to a person. Doing it in a disciplined way can be the key for you to improve your work speed over time as you become more accustomed to all of the aspects of your work process. You will know what is the best and fastest way to do something and you also understand the best approach which can bring the highest productivity on the work.

Keep on doing the work that you do should bring you faster to do it naturally. However, it might be a waste of time to do it if you spread your iterations focus in too many areas. Too much of your time will be spent on the things that mostly do not give the kind of results that you want. As you have already read the Better approach previously, you should know the important area of your work that you should focus on. The consistent iteration that you do should focus on this important area too. That way, it can improve your work speed significantly on the things that can bring a significant impact on the end results that you want from your work process.

So, you know that iteration is important to speed up your work process. However, how to keep doing the iteration on the area that matters in your work and continuously add on the know-how experience in it besides the regular work that you do? Well, you should try to force yourself to do the work which aligns itself in the area that you want to improve your productivity on. If you are an employee, then you can try to join some projects in your company which utilize the important work skill in the area or you can make yourself available to help doing some works in the kind of tasks that you want to improve on (of course, those tasks should also help you to get the end results that you want so you do not produce the work results that are not meaningful from them). If you are a business owner, then you can allocate your time as much as possible in the work that makes the business grows significantly and try to not diverse your focus into too many things because that will make you lose time to do a concentrated iteration on the area that matters. Optimize the working hours that you have in a day as much as possible and allocate them to work on the things that you feel a need to iterate should maximize the know-how experience accumulation that you have on the area that is important. Ultimately, the aim is to make you much faster in the work that you do.

In the iteration that you put in the effort for, however, there can be some struggles that you meet regarding the work which you do. There might be some points during the iteration when you think it is hard for you to do some works. When that happens, it is important to take a look at the struggles and understand whether this work experience is relevant to the productivity improvement that you aim. If they do, then you need to see the hard tasks as something that enables you to learn much more and an important roadblock that you need to overcome so you can master more things on the area that you work on. By trying to maintain that kind of mindset, you should be able to optimize your development so you can have the high productivity that you want eventually for the things that you do. Skip the hard work needed to prevail over the struggles might set you back on the aspects which are crucial to speeding up the work process significantly.

Experience is something that can never be taken away from you and as long as you keep practicing your work, you should be able to improve the way you do it and the effectivity and efficiency that you have in the process. Keep working yourself on the area that matters so you can speed up your work process over time.

FINAL WORDS: THE PRODUCTIVE HABIT

There are good habits and bad habits which can shape the condition of our life. Whatever good habits that we have, they should be something that support us to achieve a better condition in the future compared to where we are now when bad habits tend to make us fall to a bad situation. Therefore, it is crucial for us to identify what kind of good habits that we can implement consistently in our life while keeping away from the bad habits that can be harmful to us.

The Do More Better Faster approach that you have read in this book has one theme. The theme is to help you have a productive habit from applying all of the suggestions that have been given in each of the chapters on a consistent basis. This productive habit hopefully can be utilized to help you get the end results that you want from your work as soon as possible while also keeping you away from bad work habits that can make you waste your working hours. Implementing the habit surely takes time and you will need to adapt to this habit if you just begin to apply this Do More Better Faster approach. Do not relent, though, and be consistent as that is needed if you ever want to take advantage of the benefits that can be gotten by doing a positive habit in your life.

The main essence of productivity habits like the Do More Better Faster is to support you in the work that you do. Everyone who works doing it because they want to get something as a result of their work. Nobody works just for the sake of it. Therefore, if we can get the best result in the shortest period, then it will be all the better for us. Such is the reason of being productive.

In the end, the work results that we produce are be accumulated so that we can achieve success in life. Success, as we know it, mostly takes years to build and we have to work hard consistently in a long period so we are able to have a high chance to succeed. It seems that the longer hours that you work in a period, the much closer you should get to the success that you want. We can see the stories of many successful people and it seems like the long working hours is the pattern for most of them, especially in the early part of their journey to success. This also can be heard from them when they are asked how hard people should work so they can get success. Grant Cardone, a self-made millionaire, believes that you should work 95 hours a week instead of 9 to 5 to have a high chance to succeed while Gary Vaynerchuk, a very successful entrepreneur in his own right, says that you should work around 18 hours a day on your first year as an entrepreneur to build your business to the success that you want.

This is true logically because, again, the more work that you put, the more chances that you should get to have success. The people who do not work shall never be able to utilize the opportunity that they have in their life to propel them to success. However, it is always better, of course, if you can produce things fast with great quality from your work so you can achieve the success that you want much earlier.

Productivity in your work aims to reduce the time that you need to do important work significantly while also producing the best results that you can get using the resources that you have. With high productivity that you can get by implementing the Do More Better Faster approach, then it is hoped that you can succeed in a shorter time than expected.

The success that we desire can come at any age and when it does, it will be very welcomed whenever the time is in our life span. However, it is much better if it can come sooner, right? That way, we can enjoy the things that you get from the achievements much longer with the people that we love.

The journey to success is done by doing things constantly every time, one step at a time. The productive habit that you implement on your constant work should complement the outcome of it and the Do More Better Faster approach tries to support your work outcomes by trying to improve the work factors that should be important for the outcomes. The factors which are being supported are the motivation that you have for your work (Do), the amount of workload that you accomplish in a period (More), the essential works that should be done instead of wasting time on the unimportant ones (Better), and the speed that you have to finish your work without neglecting the quality factor (Faster). These four factors should produce high productivity for you because they are the things that you need in a high amount to get the best results as fast as possible. Just think about it: How can you produce your best work results if you are not even motivated to do your work? How can you give meaningful outcomes from your work if you do not work in the matters which are important and instead spend your time doing the tasks which are not relevant? How can you achieve high effectiveness and efficiency in your work if you cannot do it more and faster? All of the things which are given in the Do More Better Faster approach are essential for your work productivity.

Throughout this book, you have learned about the importance and scarcity of time resources, the mentality aspects that you need to develop to be highly productive at work, and also the things that you can do to instill the Do More Better Faster approach in your work. Now, you should understand more about why time is the only thing that you need for the success that you want and everything else that might seem to be needed for success can be achieved as long as you utilize your time for it. You also know that commitment, resiliency, consistency, desire, and curiosity are the five aspects of mentality that can support productivity particularly in doing the Do More Better Faster approach. You also get the five things that you can do for each of the four approach parts so you can work with motivation, more outputs, the right sense of importance, and faster speed. By reading all of the book contents, you should be able to have a complete understanding of why productivity is important and what you can do to improve the one that you have significantly.

However, as with all of the other self-improvement tips and tricks, the most important thing that you can do after you finish reading this book is to implement what you have already learned. Implement it consistently as the Do More Better Faster is a productive habit that should help you in navigating your work process. The first step is always the hardest. If you want to get the most out of your work, though, you must try to strengthen yourself and do as best as you can for the sake of your productivity.

As the successful people and 10,000 hours rule suggest, you must accumulate your work before you can get the success that you want. Now, begin working with high productivity, keep it consistent, and eventually, your success should come as a result of your work. Hopefully, much earlier and much better than you expect it to be.

DID YOU LIKE DO MORE BETTER FASTER?

I want to say thanks to you, the reader of this book, who has spent some of your time to read *Do More Faster Better – How to be More Productive and Get More Done in Less Time*. Hopefully, this book will serve as a strong basis for you to improve your work productivity significantly and the Do More Better Faster approach that is being introduced here can be the ideal guide that you need to implement a highly productive habit when you do the things that you have to do.

As a book author, the rating and review from the book readers are very important for me so I can see what kind of thoughts, feedbacks, or inputs that you have got regarding this book that I have written. Therefore, if you have a minute or two to spare, then do not hesitate to give your rating and review in the Amazon page where you buy this book. I will read and use them as the valuable inputs and extra motivation to write my future books!

MORE BOOKS BY DAN KRISTOPH

*****

How to Do What You Love: 3 Phases for Working with
Passion and Achieve Success

The Anti-Procrastination Mentality: How to Stop Being
Lazy and Get Things Done

Overcoming Failure: How to Turn Failure into Success

Stop Overthinking: How to Relieve Anxiety Stop Worrying
and Reduce Stress

The To-Do List Formula: The Guide to Create a To-Do
List that Improves Productivity and Makes You Achieve
Success

*****

You can see more about the books by visiting his Author
Central Page in Amazon:
http://amazon.com/author/dankristoph

ABOUT THE AUTHOR

The right self-improvement can give you a strong base to achieve what you want in life.

Do you want to be a better person and have a better life? The power of positive habits can help you significantly for that. The condition of your life seems to be created by the habits that you try to implement consistently. The positive habits can propel you to the life that you desire while the bad ones can make you stuck in a bad condition.

Having taking a liking on the subject of self-improvement, drawing the inspiration from the many books that he has read on the topic and the lessons that he has learned through his own life experience, Dan Kristoph tries to share the unique perspective that he has on self-improvement areas in each of his books. Every book that he has written contains comprehensive description and practical suggestions on what are the positive habits that can help you in many aspects of life. Hopefully by reading some of his books, you can learn and practice the habits that you need to make a better and more positive version of life that you want for yourself.

When he is not writing a book, Dan loves to read self-improvement books (obviously), watch movies, and travel. He loves to joke also though sometimes he is the only one who laughs on it :(

You can visit his blog, Positivity Stories, by visiting the below link:
http://positivitystories.com